AESCHYLUS

AESCHYLUS

THE CREATOR OF
TRAGEDY

By

GILBERT MURRAY

D.C.L., LITT.D., LL.D., F.B.A.

Formerly Regius Professor of Greek in the
University of Oxford

OXFORD
AT THE CLARENDON PRESS

Oxford University Press, Amen House, London E.C.4

GLASGOW   NEW YORK   TORONTO   MELBOURNE   WELLINGTON
BOMBAY   CALCUTTA   MADRAS   KARACHI   KUALA LUMPUR
CAPE TOWN   IBADAN   NAIROBI   ACCRA

FIRST EDITION 1940

REPRINTED LITHOGRAPHICALLY IN GREAT BRITAIN
AT THE UNIVERSITY PRESS, OXFORD, 1951, 1958
FROM SHEETS OF THE FIRST EDITION

PREFACE

SURELY there are enough, and more than enough, books on Aeschylus, not merely editions, commentaries, and translations, but literary and historical studies of the kind which the late Dr. Verrall used, somewhat disrespectfully, to call 'stuffage'? When a scholar looks at the Bodleian Catalogue, or even at his own bookshelves, it is hard to think otherwise. And yet there will be and must be more; there is no finality.

The reason is simple enough. The few very great books of the world, the books which at the end of over two thousand years have still the power to stir our pulses with their beauty and inspire our minds with the vitality of their thought, have a special value for humanity and must not be allowed to die. Yet they will die unless, generation after generation, they are studied, loved, and reinterpreted.

I remember the thrill of emotion with which, some forty years ago in the Laurentian library at Florence, I first took into my hands the great manuscript of Aeschylus, Mediceus 32, 9. They told me that Rudolf Merkel had actually wept when they gave it him; but then Merkel had just come out of prison for his part in some republican movement in Germany and it touched him to be treated with consideration and respect. He proceeded to make an extremely careful transcript of the manuscript, which was very helpful till superseded by a photographic facsimile. Others in the same situation would do something different; but every real student and lover of Aeschylus would want to do something, were it only to make notes in the margin of his book or join in the discussions of some learned society. Some would write books.

The long-suffering public has a right to make at least two minimum demands on the reinterpreter. First, he must really have studied his subject, studied it for years, before claiming that he has anything of value to say about it; secondly, he must not make his book needlessly long. I think I have satisfied both these minimum tests.

The book is not, in the stricter sense, learned. It is merely an attempt at understanding the Aeschylean plays as great literature and great drama. Such studies are apt as a class to be called 'merely popular'; and the present volume has the defects belonging to that class. It gives few references and collects no mass of evidence or authorities. It makes little or no mention of the debt I owe to previous writers. The passages quoted are mostly given in English, and taken almost always from my own published translations, a course which I recognize as open to criticism. I am conscious, however, of having resisted two temptations which might have made the book unduly long: a temptation to add argumentative footnotes explaining or defending my own views about particular passages, and a temptation to roam away from my immediate subject into other realms of literature. For instance, when showing how the great dramas and majestic style of Aeschylus had been built by him out of 'little myths and ridiculous language', it was difficult not to dilate on the similar history of such great tragedies as *Hamlet* and *Faust*: the one having grown by slow stages out of the gross jesting of Amlodhi the Fool in Scandinavian saga, traces of which still remain in Shakespeare's First Quarto; the other from the popular *Comedy of Dr. Faustus*, current in German fairs from the 16th century onwards, dealing with the fate of one who, in the words of a contemporary, was 'a fool rather than a philosopher, a vain babbler and mountebank who ought to be whipped'.

The addition of an appendix, however, and an appendix which involves some repetition of things already said, demands a word of apology. I had found in my own early reading of Greek plays that often when I imagined that I knew the play, and had my mind full of particular phrases and passages, I had in reality little conception of the play as a whole or of the dramatic value of particular scenes and junctures of scenes. This consideration applies particularly to a subtle and difficult play like the *Agamemnon*, and I am sure that the experience is common. I have seen, for example, in a linguistically competent commentary, a remark about the 'strange lack of intelligence' shown by the Elders in the Cassandra scene. The writer actually had not taken in the central thrill of the scene, that Apollo's curse was working. That is an extreme instance; but I think that many teachers, when reading, say, a speech of Clytemnestra, do not sufficiently ask themselves, or make the class ask, not merely 'What do these words mean?' but 'Why does she say that?' or 'What effect is Aeschylus aiming at here?' Such questions must be asked if we are to understand the play.

The answer we give, of course, will be conjectural and often wrong. No production of a play is perfect. I remember one of the most accomplished producers of our time telling me that, after producing Tchekhoff with marked success in London, he happened to see it played in Moscow by actors who had been trained by Tchekhoff himself, and received a shock in discovering how many points he had missed or mistaken. No doubt the shock we should receive if we could see a production of the *Agamemnon* by Aeschylus would be considerably greater. But the perfect understanding of any poem, like the perfect poem itself, is beyond the range of us mortals. We can but try our best to come near to it.

To turn back to details. As mentioned on p. 145, the continuous search for remains of Aeschylus among the broken scraps of papyrus from

Oxyrhynchus and elsewhere is occasionally re-
warded by an important find. As Mr. Lobel has
kindly let me see the fragments to be published
in his next volume, *Oxyrhynchus Papyri* XVIII,
I add this short note.

In the first place my suggestion about a
Perseus trilogy on p. 168 is proved wrong.
The new fragments of the Δικτυουλκοί, or *Net-
Drawers*, clearly belong to the same MS as the two
already published by Vitelli and Norsa in *Pap. Soc.
It.* 1209, and come from a Satyr-play, not from a
tragedy. Apparently the chest in which Danaë
and her infant were put to sea was not merely set
afloat like an open boat, but was just thrown in
with its lid nailed down. At least in the Florentine
fragment the Chorus, who are excitedly drawing
to shore some heavy object that is caught in their
net, think of it as 'a shark or whale or monster of
some kind', and in the Oxyrhynchus fragment
Danaë is said to have been 'under water' (ὕφαλος).
The Chorus are evidently Satyrs. They drag the
chest ashore, open it, and discover the mother and
child. Danaë is, apparently, asleep or unconscious. The fisherman, Dictys, is filled with pity,
promises protection to the outcasts, and bids the
Satyrs watch over them. He goes away and Danaë
awakes, to find the grotesque Satyrs dancing about
her. She makes a despairing appeal to her be-
trayer, Zeus, threatening to hang herself rather
than be thrown again into the sea or handed over

to the mercy of 'these monsters' (τοῖσΔε κνωΔάλοις).
Meantime, however, the baby is delighted with
the Satyrs' antics, and begins to laugh. They play
with it and make suitable noises (ποππυσμός), and
all goes well. In a later fragment we have a happy
ending, in which Danaë is to be married to Dictys.

One other specimen of Aeschylus' satyric style
has been found and is referred by Mr. Lobel to the
Envoys or *Isthmiastai*. The Envoys are Satyrs;
we find them outside the Temple of Poseidon
hanging up masks which are their own portraits.
(The likeness is such as would make their mother
scream!) This looks like a reference to the ritual
of the hanging *oscilla* referred to in *Georgic* ii
389 ff. (cf. the Athenian festival of Αἰώρα).
The plot is obscure. Some 'Exarchôn'—probably
Dionysus himself, since somebody calls him ἄναλκις
and γύννις—reproaches his Chorus for attending
the Isthmian festival instead of minding their own
business of dancing. Someone takes refuge inside
the temple; and some pursuer is bought off by the
gift of an object 'made by adze and anvil' of which
he does not know the use. We have no ancient
account of the plot of the *Isthmiastai*, and scholars
must be left to interpret the fragments by their
own ingenuity.

These two papyri are extremely interesting as
being the only specimens we have of the famous
Satyr-Drama of Aeschylus. Enough is left to
make one feel the grace and vigour of the style;

it seems spontaneous, high-spirited, and rapid, and
has at the same time a certain elegance about
it. But it would be rash to draw conclusions from
such slight pieces of evidence.

The new fragments of tragedy call for less comment. The Florentine papyrus of the *Niobe* is a
fine piece of Aeschylean verse. The numerous tiny
fragments of the *Glaucus of Potniae*, the third of
the *Persae* trilogy, are only tantalizing, but seem,
as Mr. Lobel points out, to fit well with the known
story of the *Sparagmos* of that hero by his own
horses. The other *Glaucus* is also represented. A
fragment of fifteen lines contains a couplet quoted
by Strabo from the *Glaucus Pontius*, and seems
to come from a speech of Glaucus telling how, in
a desert place, he found the plant of eternal life,
which we know to have been the main incident of
the play.

    Oxford.   G. M.
27 December 1939.

CONTENTS

CHAPTER I

HOW AESCHYLUS CREATED TRAGEDY

W HEN Aeschylus is called the 'creator of tragedy', it can hardly be meant that in an archaeological sense he was the first writer of Greek tragedy. There were several makers of tragedy before him, Phrynichus, Choirilus, Pratinas, and, earlier than all, Thespis. The claim made for him is a much greater one: that in the artistic or imaginative sense, he created the form of literature that we now call tragic—whether it takes shape in drama, like *Macbeth*, *Athalie*, *Faust*, or in novels, like *War and Peace* or *Les Misérables*.

Greek tragedy, strictly speaking, was a peculiar form of art with narrow limits, both local and temporary. It was, in literal meaning, a 'Goatsong', i.e. a *molpê* (dance and song combined), performed at the altar of Dionysus over the sacrifice of a dismembered goat, which, by a form of symbolism common in ancient religion, represented the god himself. Hardly acted anywhere outside one small district of Greece, lasting as a living form not much beyond the limits of the fifth century B.C., performed only at one particular type of religious festival, the Dionysia at Athens, it was associated with stage conventions derived from local religious customs which in many ways

would not bear transplanting. Its subjects might
be taken from any part of the Greek heroic
tradition; but normally the play portrayed some
traditional story which was treated as the *Aition*
or origin of some existing religious practice. For
example, if it was the custom on a certain day to
carry the coffin of Ajax to burial, with his arms
piled upon it, Sophocles would write a tragedy
representing the madness, crime, and death of
Ajax, and the great discussion about the heroic
criminal's dead body, in which by the pleading
of his old enemy Odysseus he is at last granted the
rites of honourable burial.[1] That would explain
the origin of the custom. Thus tragedy was the
product of a peculiar soil. The costume was
bizarre; the appropriate buildings, a round dancing-floor, with part of the circumference cut off
by a stage, were not to be found in many places:
the chorus of twelve—or later of fifteen—homo-
geneous persons, always present in the midst of
the most secret plots and crimes, and yet practically never doing anything to prevent them, was
almost unmanageable except in the air where it
was born; and the rich store of myths and legends

---

[1] So the *Prometheus* trilogy explains the origin of the *Promethia*;
the *Medea* that of the ritual worship of Medea's children at Corinth;
the *Hippolytus* that of the ritual weeping of virgins over the death of
Hippolytus in Trozên. Cf. Sophocles, *Electra*, 277 ff., on the mocking
Feast at Argos over a man and a woman slain by their enemies, who may
be either Agamemnon and Cassandra, or Aigisthos and Clytemnestra.
Cf. Aesch. *Ag.* 1318, 594. Also Od. γ, 308 ff.

which formed the raw material from which tragedies were made did not exist elsewhere. The whole
form of tragedy was so inflexible and so hemmed
in by tradition that it could hardly last out four
generations of poets without collapsing.

And yet its influence on the Western world has
never ceased, except at periods when the higher
culture has been submerged altogether. One
nation after another, as soon as it rose to the stage
of writing great literature at all, began to try to
write tragedy, some on the Greek model—at
least as far as they understood what the Greek
model was—and some in new ways of their own.
The Roman poets, from Ennius and Pacuvius
down to Ovid and Seneca, definitely imitated
the Greek form: Racine and Corneille did the
same: Alfieri, though different, was more formal
still. Goethe wrote *Iphigenie* in the Greek form
of tragedy and *Faust* in quite another: Shakespeare wrote tragedies in a form based on the
Greek but freely diverging from it: Milton and
Shelley and Swinburne wrote in strict and definite
imitation of the Greek. But even when the out-
ward form diverges most widely from the Greek
pattern, there is often something inward, some
spirit or essence, which enables one to say without
hesitation, not only of certain plays, but of certain
novels, or purely narrative poems, 'This is a
tragedy'. It is tragedy in this sense which seems
to me to have been created by Aeschylus.

There are, according to Aristotle, two obvious main differences between comedy and tragedy, or rather between κωμῳδία and τραγῳδία: for though our two words are descended from the Greek, their meaning has inevitably changed. In the first place, comedy is a κωμῳδία or Revel-song: it normally ends with a Kômos or Marriage-Feast; tragedy ends with a death or downfall.[1] Scholars and anthropologists now tend to agree that both forms of drama are parts of the pre-historic ritual of the Year-Daemon or Vegeta-tion-Spirit, comedy representing his triumph or marriage, tragedy his defeat and death—with perhaps a suggestion of rebirth afterwards. In the second place, Aristotle tells us, comedy is a *mimêsis* or representation of persons 'lower than ourselves', tragedy of persons higher and nobler.[2] The judgement is at first sight surprising, but can be justified by the facts. In comedy—ancient comedy was more like what we call farce—the characters are engaged in a revel or merry-making; in tragedy they are facing death, and that usually not an ordinary death, but a sacrifice.

---

[1] On this much-discussed subject I may be allowed to refer to my article on 'Greek Drama, Origins' in the *Encyclopaedia Britannica*, ed. xiv, pp. 581 ff.

[2] *Poetics* 1448ª. Βελτίονας or κρείττονας as opposed to χείρονας. Tragedy dealt almost entirely with the 'heroes'—in the Greek sense; i.e. the dead who were objects of worship. The heroes were, of course, 'greater than we', and usually 'heroic' in the modern sense.

Both forms of art, of course, want to get the full value out of their respective subjects.

'If Tragedy is to get full artistic value and beauty out of death, the death must be faced and met and somehow or other conquered on its own ground: if Comedy is to get the full value out of its revel, it must be a revel enjoyed to the full and not spoilt by any intrusive temperance or prudential considerations of the morrow. Death, to yield its full value in art, demands heroism, or some quality of the soul that can conquer death. A frolic, to yield its full value, demands a complete surrender to frolic.'[1]

It is noteworthy that tragedy even in this modern sense is almost purely a Greek form of art. Drama of one kind or another is widespread throughout the human race; but except in classical Greece and the societies influenced by Greece, you practically never find tragedy as an institution. In Indian drama the unhappy ending is actually forbidden. Presumably it would operate as a bad omen. The Chinese and Japanese dramas deal in farce, in romance, in long stories of historical adventure, but—as far as a non-expert can make out—they do not have tragedy. It is a Greek invention: the dirge or lament over the dying or suffering god gradually taking dramatic form and developing into something unknown before.

Let us stay for a moment to analyse what that something is. Greek tragedy is based on the

---

[1] *The Classical Tradition in Poetry*, p. 56.

'sufferings of Dionysus',[1] and Dionysus is one of
the many forms of the Year-god or Vegetation-
god, like Osiris, Attis, Adonis, or Thammuz. The
story of this Year-god is always the same: he is
born a miraculous child, he grows in beauty and
strength, he conquers, he wins his bride, he com-
mits the sin of *Hubris* or excess, he transgresses
the law, and thereafter must of necessity dwindle,
suffer defeat, and die. Thus the ritual of Dionysus
sees life in the tragic pattern. It is the story of
all these vegetation-gods: the story of the Sun,
the Day, and the Year: it is the story of all life;
of flower and tree, of bird and beast, of men and
of cities. All begin in beauty and frailness, grow
in strength, grow too strong or too proud, and
then inevitably dwindle and die. If we ask why
they die, the answer, it seemed to the Ancients,
must be that they die because in some sense or
other they have transgressed or sinned: death
is the wages of sin. If there were not some sin,
some error, somewhere, Aristotle tells us, the
calamitous ending would be μιαρόν, 'wicked'
or 'revolting'. This, then, is life seen in the
tragic pattern: a splendid thing growing but
doomed.

Such an account is perhaps enough to give us
tragedy in the full sense, without any further
addition. Yet there is, I think, a further factor in

[1] Hdt. v. 67. Πάθεα means strictly the 'things that happened to'
Dionysus.

the Year-ritual which may be of very great importance. This celebration of the Death of the Year-god takes place not in the autumn but in the early spring. A fragmentary form of the Year-ritual survives even now in northern and eastern Europe under the name of the Mummers' Play, in which the hero goes through various battles and ordeals; and one cannot help noticing that after his death he is often restored to life by a Wizard or Learned Doctor, or sometimes by the enemy who has just killed him. This might be explained as due to a mere popular wish for a happy ending, were it not that the same resurrection or restoration to life occurs in the Egyptian myth and many of the ancient Greek myths, and also is an obvious fact in the story of the Year itself. The Year dies, but is immediately born again and proceeds through the same cycle. The dead Osiris is sought for, discovered, and restored; so are Dionysus, Adonis, Asclepius. Even where beings of this type are not actually restored to life they are made into heroes and receive ritual worship at their tombs, like Hippolytus, have temples like Menelaus and Helen, or are admitted into Olympus itself, like Dionysus and Heracles. That is to say, the conception of a triumph over Death, which we found on artistic grounds to be essential to tragedy, seems to be latent in the original dirge-ritual itself. It is a funeral lamentation for a dead hero, yet from the very beginning there seems to have been some consciousness, or some suggestion, that Death was not really the end. In its primitive form this victory over death demands the definite resurrection or rebirth of the hero; in its higher form it is the feeling which finds such magnificent expression in the last speech of Milton's *Samson Agonistes*, that whether the hero is dead or no, he has in some deeper sense actually conquered the evil to which his body succumbed, and that 'nothing is here for tears'.

This, I think, is the characteristic of Greek tragedy, and the explanation of its undying influence. Most nations, in contemplating life through the drama, have insisted on having pleasant stories or at least happy endings. They preferred not to look on the darker sides of life, and thereby for the time could forget them. But the fifth-century Greeks were ready to look straight at its most awful possibilities, to show men terrified by them, struggling with them, overthrown and destroyed by them, so long as by some loftiness in the presentation or some nobility in the characters or perhaps some sheer beauty and inspiration in the poetry, one could feel in the end not defeat but victory, the victory of the spirit of man over the alien forces among which he has his being.

There is a lyric of Euripides in the *Medea* consciously claiming this power for tragedy. Why did the bards of old, he asks, waste their music

on festivals and occasions of joy? When men are
happy they do not need poetry, and as a matter
of fact do not much listen to it.

> But all the darkness and the wrong,
>   Quick deaths and dim heart-aching things,
> Would no one ease them with a song
>   And music of a thousand strings?
> Then song had helped us in our need. . . .[1]

That, then, is what I understand tragedy to be:
the song or fiction that does deal with 'quick
deaths and dim heart-aching things', and vouch-
safes us the revelation—or maybe the illusion—
that there are other values accessible to man,
beyond the obvious values of physical life or
death, of happiness or suffering, and that in
attaining them the spirit of man can and does
conquer death. It is of tragedy in that sense that
I think Aeschylus may justly be considered the
creator.

Now let us turn to the man himself. It will
perhaps be convenient to begin by noting briefly
the main dates of his life, so far as they are known
to us.

His first victory in one of the official competi-
tions at the Dionysia was in the year 484 B.C.
This date is fairly certain, since the contests were
regularly recorded at the time and the records were
afterwards collected and published by Aristotle.

---

[1] *Medea*, 195 ff.

His first play is said by Suidas to have been produced in the 70th Olympiad, i.e. between 500
and 497 B.C. As to his birth, it is not likely to
have been recorded; but the convention in ancient
historiography is to choose some date as a man's
acme or *floruit*, and then, if there is no conflicting
evidence, to assume that when he 'flourished' he
was forty years of age. Now Aeschylus presumably 'flourished' when he won his first victory in
484. Consequently we find his birth put by the
Parian Chronicle forty years earlier, in 525–524
B.C.[1] We have also two definite dates at the end of
his life. He produced his masterpiece, the *Oresteia*, in 458 B.C., and died at Gela in Sicily two
years later, in 456.

We have thus the following set of dates:

524 Aeschylus born.

500? Produced his first play.

490 Fought in the heavy-armed infantry at the
Battle of Marathon. About this time, or pos-
sibly even earlier, produced the *Suppliant
Women*, the earliest of his extant plays.

484 Won his first victory: name of the play not
known.

480, 479 Fought at Salamis and Plataea?

476 In Syracuse; produced the '*Aetna*', or '*Women of
Aetna*', at the foundation of that city by Hiero.
Probably soon afterwards produced the *Pro-
metheus*, which mentions (v. 367) an eruption of
Mt. Etna. A great eruption occurred, according

---

[1] Either 525–524 or 524–523, being sixty-nine at death and thirty-
five at the Battle of Marathon.

to the Parian marble, in 479 B.C. (According to Thucydides (iii. 116) it was 'fifty years before' the eruption of 425. This would mean 475, but Thucydides may be using round numbers.)

472 Produced the *Persae*; Pericles was Choregus for him this year.[1]

471–469 Made a second journey to Sicily, to produce the *Persae* there (ἀναδιδάξαι τοὺς Πέρσας).

468 Was defeated for the first time; by Sophocles.

467 Produced the *Seven against Thebes*.

458 Produced his masterpeice, the *Oresteia*.

456 Died at Gela in Sicily.

The seven plays which are still extant represent, apparently, about a tenth part of his work, or less. Our information on the subject is contradictory, but we know the titles of some seventy-nine plays, of which at least thirteen were not tragedies but satyr-plays. Aeschylus was a prolific and successful writer. The ancient 'Life of Aeschylus' says he won thirteen victories in his lifetime and 'many more' after his death. The article in Suidas' *Lexicon*, perhaps adding these in, gives him twenty-eight victories.

It is interesting to note something of his family history. It was, or at least became, a highly theatrical family. He himself was the son of Euphorion of Eleusis. He had two sons, one Euphorion, of whom nothing is known, one Euaion, whose name, curiously enough, is pre-

---

[1] See *C.I.G.* II, 971; Wilhelm, *Urkunden Dramatischer Ausfuhr-üngen in Athen*, p. 18; Wilamowitz in *Hermes*, xxi. 614.

served on some contemporary vases with the word
καλός ('beautiful') attached. The Athenians considered it unseemly to give public praise to women
for their good looks, but apparently thought it
did no harm to young men. That is all we know
of Aeschylus' own descendants, but his brother
and his sister are both interesting. The brother,
Kynegeiros, met a famous death at the Battle of
Marathon, where he had his arm cut off by an axe
while trying to drag back one of the Persian boats.[1]
The sister's name is not recorded and we know
nothing of her character, but she seems to have
been the means of carrying on the family genius
to future generations. Her son Philocles wrote
tragedies and actually won the first prize against
Sophocles' masterpiece, the *Oedipus Tyrannus*.
His son was Morsimus, who obtained some tragic
prize in 424 and is sometimes chaffed by Aristophanes; his son again was Astydamas, who won a
prize for tragedy in 392. Astydamas had two
playwrights for sons, the first called Philocles, the
second, a very successful writer, Astydamas the
Second. One Astydamas—it is uncertain whether
the first or the second—had a great victory in 372
with a play called *Parthenopaios*, after which he
was granted the special honour of a statue in the
theatre precinct. He asked and obtained permis-

---

[1] Hdt. vi. 114. Another brother was Ameinias, but seems not to
be identical with 'Ameinias of Pallene', who distinguished himself at
Salamis. Hdt. viii. 84 and 93.

sion to write the inscription on the statue himself; and—such are the cruel traps that Providence
lays in the path of impulsive artists—he wrote one
in such enthusiastic terms that it had to be taken
down, while a more sober statement was put in
its place by the proper authorities.[1] A sad end
to the five successive generations of tragic poets
sprung from Euphorion!

As to Aeschylus himself, in order to have our
feet on firm ground let us start with two or three
of the definite statements of the ancient Greeks
themselves about the early stages of tragedy and
about Aeschylus as its creator. In the *Frogs* of
Aristophanes there is a famous contest in the
shades between Aeschylus and Euripides. Most
of it is on points of technique, but the opening
deals with the general character of the two poets,
Aeschylus representing the older style of poetry
and Euripides the new. Aeschylus at his first
appearance is greeted with the words: 'O thou who
first of the Greeks didst build majestic words into
towers and create a world (*cosmos*) of tragic humbug.'[2] He built towers of majestic words (ῥήματα
σεμνά), and made a Cosmos, an ordered world,

---

[1] Cf. Suidas, s.v. Ἀστυδάμας and Σαυτὴν ἐπαινεῖς. Diodorus,
xiv. 33.

[2] Cf. Ar. *Frogs*, 1004 f. ἀλλ' ὦ πρῶτος τῶν Ἑλλήνων πυργώσας
ῥήματα σεμνά | καὶ κοσμήσας τραγικὸν λῆρον. Aristotle, *Poet.* 1449ᵃ
20 (ἡ τραγῳδία) ἐκ μικρῶν μύθων καὶ λέξεως γελοίας διὰ τὸ ἐκ σατυ-
ρικοῦ μεταβαλεῖν ὀψε ἀπεσεμνύνθη, and a little earlier πολλὰς μετα-
βολὰς μεταβαλοῦσα ἡ τραγῳδία ἐπαύσατο ἐπεὶ ἔσχε τὴν αὑτῆς φύσιν.

of the 'humbug' or illusions of the tragic stage (τραγικὸν λῆρον).

Take that in connexion with Aristotle's statement that Tragedy 'starting from small myths and ridiculous diction did not achieve majesty (ἀπεσεμνύνθη) till late'. Presumably that σεμνότης or 'majesty' was the work of him who was the first to build those towers of 'majestic words'. If we follow the scene in the *Frogs* a little farther, we shall find much about the Aeschylean σεμνότης, both in diction and in costume. But there is also some insistence on σεμνότης in human character. Aeschylus asks Euripides:

Pray tell me on what particular ground a poet should claim admiration.

EURIPIDES

If his art is true and his counsel sound: and if he brings help to the nation,
By making men better in some respect.

AESCHYLUS

And if you have done the reverse,
And had upon good strong men the effect of making them weaker and worse?
What do you say should your recompense be?

DIONYSUS

The gallows. You needn't ask him.

AESCHYLUS

Then think what they were when he had them from me!
Good six-footers, solid of limb,
Well born, well bred, not ready to fly from obeying their country's call

Nor in latter-day fashion to loiter and lie and keep their
consciences small. . . .

Aeschylus continues to expound the military
qualities of his plays, how they nerved people to
deeds of daring:

For observe, from the world's first start,
Those poets have all been of practical use who have
been supreme in their art.

He shows this in the cases of Orpheus, Musaeus,
Hesiod, and above all, of Homer.

And in his great spirit my plays had a part, with their
heroes many and brave,
Teucers, Patrocluses, lions at heart, who made my
citizens crave
To dash like them at the face of the foe, and leap to
the call of a trumpet.
But no Stheneboia I've given you, no; no Phaedra, no
heroine-strumpet!
If I've once put a woman in love in one act of one play
may my teaching be scouted!

EURIPIDES
No, you hadn't exactly the style to attract Aphrodite.

AESCHYLUS
I'm better without it.

We shall have occasion later to refer to many
particular points in this famous scene; for the
present I would only remark that throughout the
whole of it the characteristic of Aeschylus is
dignity or majesty (σεμνότης). Here it is dignity

of character; later on, majesty of diction and of
stage dress. The chief difficulty in using the scene
for our present purpose is that it aims at contrast-
ing Aeschylus with a later stage of tragedy whereas we want to contrast him with something earlier.
We want to see what he did to tragedy, not how
subsequent poets did something different.

In the first place, then, Aeschylus made
tragedy σεμνόν.

In the second place, he took part in the general
technical development of tragedy. About this
subject Aristotle has some very characteristic re-
marks to make. He conceives the history of
tragedy as an evolution or development towards
the attainment of a natural end or perfection.
And this perfection of form he regards as having
been reached before his own time. 'Tragedy', he
says, 'began no doubt from improvisations. It
advanced little by little, as the artists made such
improvements as they could think of': or literally,
'drew forward as much of it as they could see'.
(That is to say, by implication: the perfect form
of tragedy existed potentially, and the artists
caught glimpses from time to time of what it
might be, and 'drew forward' or 'brought out'
what they saw.) He continues: 'It was after a long
series of changes that Tragedy attained its natural
form, and changed no more.' Evidently it did
not reach that perfect form in the hands of
Aeschylus, because he continues: 'The number of

actors was increased to two instead of one by Aeschylus, who also reduced the importance of the Chorus and made the dialogue take the leading part. A third actor and scenery were due to Sophocles.'

There is some difficulty about these last words, because Aeschylus certainly does sometimes use three actors and very emphatically he uses scenic effects. One can only suppose that Aristotle means that Sophocles was the first to use three actors, though Aeschylus followed his example, and that the kind of scenery which was standardized in Aristotle's time was due to Sophocles. This last point leads to some extremely interesting results, in which Greek drama shows a contrast to Elizabethan. Whereas on the whole Shakespeare, like Ibsen, gets bolder as he goes on, and makes greater and greater demands on his scene-painters, Greek drama seems to have done the opposite. We find Aeschylus groping round for great scenic effects and trying bold fantastic experiments which in later days proved not suitable for the Greek tragic stage and were discarded in favour of a more modest setting.

A third point of great importance for appreciating Aeschylus is not stated directly in any ancient text, and is not perhaps sufficiently stressed in the histories of literature. It is that the Greek tragedians as a whole were poets of ideas, and of bold ideas; poets like Milton or Shelley or Goethe or Victor Hugo, not like Shakespeare, Scott, Ovid, or the Homeric poets. True to the religious origin of the Dionysiac Festival, they practically always find in the myths which form their raw material some deep religious or eternal meaning. Tragedy deals with *res sacra*, not merely in conventional form but in reality. In Aeschylus especially, the thoughts about man and the world which he had to put forth in his plays were an important part of his inspiration; in other words, he cared greatly about philosophic or religious truth, as well as about beauty, and used his art for expounding it. His emotions were stirred by the world of intellect as well as the world of sense and fantasy.

A contrary conception of Aeschylus is generally predominant, I think, and seems to be due to a somewhat careless reading of the contest in the *Frogs*. Euripides, as the poet of ideas and of new ideas, *par excellence*, is there contrasted with Aeschylus: and one is liable in consequence to think of Aeschylus as the poet of pure poetry, uninterested in ideas, or the merely conservative poet, whose ideas, if he has any, are old. But I believe that the contrast is really between two poets who are both of them teachers and thinkers, but who represent two different ages. Aeschylus represents the ideas, as well as the technique, of the age which built up the greatness of Athens and created tragedy; Euripides those which,

coming after the solvent influences of the Sophistic
movement and the long disillusionment of the
Peloponnesian War, seemed to Aristophanes to
point to the fall of Athens and the disintegration
of tragedy. If Aristophanes had wanted to contrast Euripides the sophist-poet with a pure poet
not interested in philosophy, he would, I think,
have taken Sophocles, not Aeschylus, for the
purpose. As it is he deliberately leaves Sophocles
aside, as εὔκολον μὲν ἐνθάδ᾽, εὔκολον 𝛿᾽ ἐκεῖ, a being
unruffled by these disputations.

Let us try then to notice in Aeschylus these
three characteristics: first, his gift of *Semnotês*,
bringing greatness or majesty where it was not
before; next, his bold experimentation in stage
technique in directions which were not followed
afterwards by classical tragedy; and thirdly, his
intellectual vividness as a thinker stirred by great
ideas.

To begin with the first of these, we may take
the *Prometheus Bound* and consider what raw
material Aeschylus found to his hand when he
set to work to make that tragedy. He would find
his material chiefly in the local Athenian worship
of a petty daemon called Prometheus, who was a
trade patron of the potters and the smiths. We
know that he was worshipped together with
Hephaistos at a common altar, which is sometimes called simply 'the Altar of Prometheus',
partly because he was the older of the two, partly

no doubt because it was the only one he had, whereas Hephaistos had many.[1] The chief incident in his worship was a torch-race at the feast called 'Promethia' or 'Hephaistia'. The torches were lit at the Altar of Erôs at the entrance of the Academy. The race started from the Altar of Prometheus. It went through the inner and outer Kerameikos, or Potters' Quarter, and home.

We find thus (1) that Prometheus is a local fire-god, patron of certain trades; (2) that he was 'older', i.e. more primitive, than Hephaistos, but that otherwise they were closely akin. Both, for instance, are said to have taught men the use of fire, to have been founders of human culture, to have delivered Athena from the head of Zeus.[2] Again, Prometheus, like Hephaistos, was one of the Kabeiroi, who were primitive phallic daemons and generally dwarfs. They were connected with 'mysteries', that is, with the somewhat undignified and primitive initiation ceremonies of the indigenous population.[3]

So far we are on safe ground, but we may, by conjecture, reach a little farther. It is extremely common in Greek mythology to find that a legend has taken its rise from the misinterpretation of

---

[1] κοινὴ βάσις Schol. Soph. *O.C.* 57; Paus. i. 30. 2.

[2] Harpoc. λαμπάς; Diod. v. 74; *Hym. Hom.* 20; Eur. *Ion,* 455.

[3] The objects found at the Kabeiros sanctuary near Thebes are in a style of 'broad humour and caricature' (Frazer). Paus. ix. 25. 6.

some work of art.[1] The smith-god Hephaistos
was represented with a hammer and chain. What
can they mean? The myth-maker idly turns
them into a story. They are for use upon
Hephaistos' altar-companion Prometheus, who
was a Titan, i.e. a god of the older dynasty conquered by Zeus, and therefore likely to receive
some kind of punishment. Hence he is *Prometheus Desmôtes*, Prometheus Bound. But as 'Fire-
God' Hephaistos or Prometheus had perhaps also
an eagle with him, a regular symbol of fire.
'Why an eagle?' asks the legend-maker. Presumably the eagle is there to devour Prometheus
as part of his punishment. But further, if he is
punished, he must have done something wrong.
The same question arises as about Sisyphus,
Tantalus, Salmôneus, and other well-known sinners. They must have been very bad because we
know of their sufferings in Tartarus, but, unfortunately, no one is quite sure what they did.
One suggestion is based on the fact that Prometheus was represented as carrying fire hidden
in a hollow reed. That is, he taught men how to
make fire by twisting a hard stick rapidly round
and round inside a soft reed or bulrush. (It may
be noticed in passing that Dr. Kuhn has pointed
out that the name Prometheus is a correct Greek
derivative from the Sanskrit *Pramantha* which

---

[1] See Reinach's famous article on 'Sisyphe aux Enfers et quelques
autres Damnés', *Cultes, Mythes et Religions*, ii. 159 ff.

means 'Fire-stick'. If so, of course the word has been worked over in Greek, so as to seem like 'forethinker', and the 'Forethinker' has been provided with a brother 'Epimetheus', the 'Afterthinker'.) Now, why did he hide fire in a reed? If he hid it he must have been stealing it. But why did he want to steal it at all? The reason is simple. As a potter, he had moulded man out of clay, and he wanted to put the fire of life inside him:[1] making him 'like a god, knowing good and evil'; and of course Zeus would not stand that. Then again, since he was a fire-god, he probably originated the custom of burnt sacrifice. Now the arrangement of a Greek burnt sacrifice was rather peculiar. The gods received the bones and the superfluous fat while the worshippers themselves consumed the flesh. Clearly the worshippers had the best of it. How was Zeus ever induced to accept such an arrangement? Clearly it was Prometheus himself who deceived him. It was just the sort of thing for a cunning fire-dwarf to do; and so, of course, Zeus punished him. That is the material that Aeschylus found in the local cult and, as far as we can conjecture, in the local folk-tales.

What was there if he looked beyond? The

---

[1] This form of the story is implied in Hesiod and assured by the connexion of the Promethia with the Kerameikos: cf. Ar. *Av.* 686 πλάσματα πήλου; else the first explicit authority is Erinna 4 (if genuine), cf. Phaedr. iv. 14A. Hor. *Carm.* 1. iii is the first mention of his adding fire, i.e. soul, to the clay, but this must have been in the original story.

story of Prometheus was told in more or less canonical form by Hesiod. If we read it, we shall find that in the main it is the same story of this old patron of the potters, the cunning smith and fireworker, though it is told in a sort of mock-heroic language, which uses all the sonorous epithets and periphrases of the Homeric style. It is difficult at this distance of time to know how far this Hesiodic magniloquence was intended to be ornamental, or how far it was really meant to raise a smile. But one is certainly reminded of Aristotle's phrase about the λέξις γελοία, the 'laughable diction' from which tragedy began.[1]

'When gods and mortal men were at strife in Mêkônê, Prometheus with eager heart set forth a great ox which he had divided so as to deceive the mind of Zeus. The flesh and entrails rich in fat he covered with the paunch and put them inside the hide, but the white bones of the ox he laid out cunningly covered with gleaming fat. Then said the Father of gods and men: "Friend, how unfairly thou hast divided the portions!" And crafty Prometheus answered, gently smiling, while he forgot not his cunning: "O Zeus, most great and glorious of the immortal gods, choose whichever of them thy spirit bids." And Zeus with both hands took up the gleaming fat. And there was wrath in his breast, yea, rage fell upon his spirit, when he saw the white bones of the ox in that cunning device. (And from that time forth the race of man doth burn to the gods on their fragrant altars the bones of the victims.) Then spake Zeus the cloud-

---

[1] Hesiod. *Theog.* 536 ff., but cf. the whole passage 520–616.

gatherer in heavy wrath: "Son of Iapetos, who knowest devices beyond all, thou hast not forgotten yet thy guileful way."

'And thereafter, ever remembering that craft, he gave not to unhappy men[1] the force of unwearied fire; but the good Prometheus outwitted him, by stealing the far gleam of untiring fire in a hollow reed. And Zeus the high-thunderer was stung within him, and wrath was in his heart when he saw among men the gleam of fire far-visible. And straightway, to make up for the fire, he made an evil thing for man. . . . [Then comes an account of Pandora, the woman.] Thus it is not possible to deceive or outstrip the mind of Zeus; for not even the Son of Iapetos, the benefactor Prometheus, escaped his heavy wrath, but perforce for all his subtlety great bonds hold him down.'[2]

The story of Pandora is told more fully in the *Works and Days*.[3] Prometheus stole the fire and gave it to man.

---

[1] Reading μελέοισι in default of a satisfactory explanation of μελίησι.

[2] A little earlier comes the account of his punishment, 520 ff. 'He bound in harsh fetters Prometheus of many wiles, in cruel bondage, driving a stake through his midst, and set upon him a long-winged eagle. It devoured his liver, which was immortal, and during the night there grew as much as the long-winged bird had eaten in all the day. Him the bold son of Alcmena (Heracles) slew, and warded off the fell affliction from Prometheus and set him free from his pains, not against the will of Zeus the high counsellor, who sought that the fame of Theban Heracles should be wider yet over the bounteous earth.' The words μέσον διὰ κίον' ἐλάσσας might also mean 'driving him through the middle of a (wooden) post', i.e. making fire a prisoner inside the wood. The story would no doubt be clearer to us if we knew what the figure on the 'common altar' was like.

[3] Hes. *Erga*, 42 ff., esp. 59 ff.

'To him in wrath spoke the cloud-compeller: "Son of Iapetos, crafty beyond all, art thou glad that thou hast stolen fire and beguiled my heart, a deed that means great evil to thee and to men hereafter? To make up for fire I will give them an evil thing, wherein they shall rejoice, hugging their own bane."

'So spake the Father of gods and men, and laughed aloud; and he bade the famous Hephaistos with all speed mix earth and water, and put into it human voice and strength and make it like an immortal goddess to look upon, a lovely maiden shape; and he bade Athena teach it woman's works and the weaving of subtle webs; and the golden Aphrodite to pour delight about its head and heavy longing and cares that consume the limbs; and Hermes the Argos-slayer to put therein a dog's mind and the heart of a thief.'

Then follows the acceptance of Pandora by Epimetheus, and the obscure story of the casket which she opened.

Thus, the story which lay before Aeschylus tells of a contest of wits between Zeus and the cunning old fire-daemon, in which of course Zeus has the last word. Prometheus deceives Zeus in the division of the burnt sacrifice; Zeus says there shall be no more burnt sacrifices and takes away fire from man. Prometheus steals fire for man 'in a hollow reed'; that is, when there is no visible fire left anywhere in the world, he knows that there is really fire hidden in the soft wood of a reed if you rub it enough with a fire-stick; Zeus then says, 'You have given men fire, I will give them something worse than fire',[1] and gave them the first woman. It is all on the level of common folk-lore, light myth-making combined with the misinterpretation of the old fire-daemon's attributes as marks of punishment.

Now what does Aeschylus make of this very trivial and unimpressive story?

He drops the undignified quarrel about the dividing of the burnt sacrifice. He drops the rustic wit about Pandora. The only relic of her is a couplet (252 f.) which mentions that Prometheus saved men from 'thoughts of death'. How?

PROM. Blind hopes I planted in their hearts to dwell.
CHOR. A blessed thing for lives so miserable.

The whole ground of strife is that Prometheus gave man fire, and we soon find that it was not ordinary fire, but fire from heaven.

But Prometheus himself had first to be transfigured. He was a Titan, a god of the older generation; but these older gods have been transformed from mere undignified phallic daemons into something dark and great. If they were conquered, it was because they were too ancient and simple-minded to stand against the deep-laid plots of their young conqueror. Prometheus, however, was different from the rest: he was the Forethinker; he saw that Zeus with his power of intellect must prevail, and tried to warn his brethren:

---

[1] Cf. Eur. *fr.* 429 ἀντὶ πυρὸς γὰρ ἄλλο πῦρ μεῖζον ἐβλάστομεν γυναῖκες, πολὺ δυσμαχώτερον.

But no power to me was given
To move the brood Titanic, born of Earth
And Sky. All crooked thoughts they turned to mirth
In their great hearts, and thought full easily
By strength to conquer all.

Prometheus gave up the attempt and supported Zeus in the great war. At the end of it, when Zeus had settled accounts with his divine enemies, he looked about him and saw with disgust the race of men, so blind, so suffering and futile, and determined to wipe them out of existence. Prometheus loved mankind and resolved to save them. To do so he stole the fire of heaven and gave it to man: the fire without gave man mastery over every art and craft, the fire within gave him a soul. Man had, as it were, eaten of the tree of knowledge and a heavenward road lay open before him. For that Zeus chained Prometheus in eternal bondage to a crag in the Scythian desert, his breast transfixed by a blade of adamant.

The play begins with a scene where Hephaistos, with Zeus' two attendant daemons, Might and Force, is sent to bind him.

MIGHT

Here on the world's last verge our feet are set,
The Scythian's zone, unearthly, desolate.
Hephaistos, now bethink thee of the charge
Our father on thee laid, against the marge
Of this sky-piercing precipice to bind
In gyves of adamant and bondage blind

This Wrecker of the Law. 'Twas he who stole
Fire, thine own glory, fire which is the soul
Of every art, and flung to men away.
For which sin to all heaven he needs must pay
Atonement, till he learn our Master's plan
To accept, and cease this love for mortal man.

HEPHAISTOS

O Force and Might, to you the word of Jove
Is all in all. Against it naught may move.
But my heart sickens, in this craggy high
And tempest-riven gulf to crucify
A god, my kinsman. . . . Yet I needs must find
The heart to do it. Woe to him whose mind
Shrinks from its task beneath the eternal eyes! . . .

(*Turning to* PROMETHEUS)

O Child of Themis, meek as she was wise,
Thou dreamer all too daring, though my heart
Is loath as thine, I shall perform my part,
Aye, and in bonds of brass indissoluble
Nail thee against this life-deserted hill,
Where never face of man, nor voice, nor name
Shall reach thee; scorchèd in the mid-day flame
Thy scaling flesh shall blacken. Thou shalt cry
For spangle-sleevèd Night to veil that eye
Of fire, shalt cry again for dawn to fold
Back from thy limbs night's agonies of cold.
Alway the present pain shall be the one
Most hated; and redeemer hast thou none.
    Lo, the reward of all thy love for man!
Thou, born of Heaven, hast heeded not the ban
Of Heaven, but given a power beyond the right
To them that perish. Therefore, day and night,
This joyless crag alway shall cradle thee,
Erect, not closing eye nor bending knee.

Aye, many a groan and cry shalt utter there,
All fruitless; Jove's heart listeth not to prayer. . .
But conquerors all are hard in the early days.

The whole difference of atmosphere is manifest. The transfiguration has taken place.

In detail it will be noticed that Aeschylus has made some small changes. He has added to Zeus the two ministers or attendants who, in another passage of the *Theogony* (385 ff.), are said never to leave him, wherever he moves or sits. They are Kratos and Bia, Kratos meaning Might or Victory, and Bia Force or Violence. Aeschylus accepts them as the true emblems of the tyrant.

At a later point he introduces to the story a new figure, strange, romantic, and perhaps mystical, who seems at first sight to have nothing to do with it. This is the horned Moon-maiden, Io, daughter of Inachus, pursued by the lust of Zeus, driven over the world by the stings of a gad-fly, by maddening music, and by the ghost of the hundred-eyed Argos ever on the watch to see that she shall not escape. She comes at last to where Prometheus hangs in chains, and we recognize her as his fellow victim.

10

What land? What people? Who is he
  Whom thus in bridle-curb of stone
  I see storm-beaten? . . . What hast done
So dire that here they torture thee?
  Answer; and say to what strange zone
I have wandered in my misery.

Ah, Ah!
  Again some gad-fly blade
Stabs me. Ah, ghost of earth-born Argos, back!
Hold him, O Mother Earth! I am afraid.
    There with a thousand eyes
He comes . . . on, on. Crafty he is and black,
  And though he is dead, long dead, he never lies
Quiet in the grave. He still will rise, will rise,
Up from the dead, a bloodhound, hunting me
Along the sands, beside the starving sea.

I cannot sleep. The wax-enwoven reed
Pipes on. Oh, whither do these wild ways lead,
    So far, so far? What sin,
O Thou Eternal, didst thou find in me,
    What wickedness within,
To bind on me this yoke of agony
    And madness; and my head
    Pierced with this stabbing dread?
Oh, kill me! Burn me with thy fire; or heap
Earth on my lips, or fling me to the deep
    To feed the monsters there!
Have mercy, Master, on thy servant's prayer!
    I am so heavy-laden
With weariness, and know not where to fly
    From this long misery.
Oh, hear me; it is I, thy hornèd Maiden!

Last but not least important, Aeschylus makes
use of a story told at the beginning of the *Theogony* about the successive kings who have ruled
Heaven and been displaced by their sons. The
story is clearly derived from the traditional Year-
cult. First Ouranos is king; then he is overthrown
by a son stronger than himself, Kronos. Then

Kronos in turn is overthrown by his son Zeus. Now Zeus reigns, but is that the end of the story? In Hesiod there is nothing more. But in Aeschylus Prometheus has learnt from his mother, the Prophetess Themis or Gaia—'many names for one eternal form'—the secret on which the reign of Zeus depends. If Zeus carries out his purpose of wedding the sea-spirit Thetis, he will fall, because it is fated that Thetis shall bear a son greater than his father. By adding this factor Aeschylus gives Prometheus a weapon which, in the end, if he can hold out, will give him the victory over Zeus. It is the will to endure pitted against the will to crush.

Prometheus pours out his heart to the Chorus when alone with them.[1]

> I swear that yet, for all his stubborn pride,
> Zeus shall bow low his head. There is a bride
> He woos and wins; and, winning, shall be hurled
> From that high throne and sceptre of the world
> To darkness. Then the curse shall be complete
> Which, falling conquered from the aeonian seat,
> Our father, Kronos, spake. To avert that hour
> Is mine alone: no other god hath power:
> I know what comes and how. So let him there
> Sit joyous, trusting in the thunder-blare
> That rolls on high, and ever in his hand
> Grasping the death-fire of his levin-brand:
> Shall these avail him on that day when he
> Must fall, dishonoured, irrecoverably
> To the great deep?

[1] 907 ff.

He answers the threats of Hermes, the messenger of Zeus, with defiance (953 ff.).

Aye, haughty-lipped thy speech, and thy heart brave
With boasting, as befits the Olympians' slave.
I read you well, young gods and new in power,
And dreaming, thronèd in a griefless tower
To reign for evermore. Have I not known
From that same tower two monarchs overthrown?
And yet the third shall know, in shame most dire,
Most sudden. Thinkest thou I dread the ire
Of these young gods, or cower to them? Not so.
  Begone the way thou camest! Thou shalt know
From me no word. of what thou questionest.

In answer Zeus hurls him to the abyss.

That is perhaps enough to illustrate our first point, how in the 'little myths and ridiculous diction' which lay before him Aeschylus found deeper values and a hidden majesty: how he 'built great words into towers' and produced tragedy.

But the *Prometheus* does not stand alone in this respect. The actual ideas of Aeschylus in the *Prometheus* and his solution of the strife between God and man's conscience will be considered later. Io herself can provide us with another example of this transfiguration.

The very earliest Greek play that has come to us, the *Suppliant Women*, is based on just such another piece of half-childish, half-humorous folklore. It is one of those stories whose childishness makes a Greek scholar feel puzzled and slightly ashamed. The way in which I can understand

such folk-tales best is by imagining the peasants
in their villages lying idly in the sun, or sitting
round the fire at night, and letting their fancies
roam, as they talked over all the questions that
were suggested by natural phenomena, by old
customs, or by the many heroic works of art and
architecture that remained from the great days
of the Minoan or Mycenaean empires (Cf. note
on p. 233). They watched the hornèd Moon
flying across the sky through hurrying clouds. . . .
Io they called her in Argos. . . . What was she,
and why did she fly so fast? A hornèd maiden,
obviously; or perhaps a cow, or both; she fled
from some pursuer, doubtless an unwelcome lover;
perhaps from Zeus, the great Bull-god. One could
see her hiding behind the clouds, but she could
never stay hidden because of the stars, the

> innumerable, pitiless, passionless eyes

from which there was no escape. The explanation
is that of the Greeks themselves, not the conjecture
of a modern mythologist.

Other fables came, as suggested above, from
fanciful misinterpretations of the monuments of
ancient kings, the terrible aliens who had once
been tyrants in Hellas. Our peasants could see on
Acro-Corinth, where a citadel had been built on
the top of a very steep hill, a sculpture, like certain
Assyrian sculptures, showing the great builder
Sisyphus planting his stone on the crest of the hill.
Doubtless it was his punishment; for ever he must

push up that monstrous stone, and at the end it will
always roll down. Another great king, Tantalus,
is shown sitting in his beautiful garden under the
fruit trees; what punishment was that? Ah, you
may notice the fruit is just out of his reach, he can
never touch it; there is water beneath him, but
will it be there if he stoops to it? No, he will never
drink. Similarly, there were female figures, the
Daughters of Danaus, who were representatives
of the innumerable streams that watered the marsh
of Argolis; like other river-gods, they were sculp-
tured as carrying urns from which the water ran.
That too was turned in the peasant's fancy into a
punishment: an eternal carrying of water in per-
forated vessels, from which the water eternally
slipped away: endless labour unavailing.

What had all these sinners done to deserve such
hard sentences? Just as with Prometheus, you will
find the answers rather shifting and uncertain.
They must have done something very bad; that
is clear; but the tradition is never quite certain
what it was. They betrayed a secret of Zeus, they
boasted against the gods, they gave somebody his
son's flesh to eat, they murdered their husbands:
who knows? No doubt they deserved all they got.

Danaus, coming from Egypt, was the culture
hero of Argolis. His chief title to fame is that he
'found the land parched and made it well watered'.[1]

---

[1] Ἄργος ἄνυδρον ἐὸν Δάναος ποίησεν ἔνυδρον Hes. fr. 24 Rzach, or
as Strabo has it, Ἄργος ἄνυδρον ἐὸν Δανααὶ θέσαν Ἄργος ἔνυδρον.

He did this by means of his daughters, who were rivulets, many rivulets—in round numbers, say, fifty. The waters of the Argive marsh were stagnant and sterile until he had them, as it were, wedded and made fruitful by channelling, as the Egyptians made the Delta fruitful by channelling the waters of the Nile.

In this or some similar way we obtain the folklore myth that the fifty Sons of the Nile or of Egypt pursued the fifty Daughters of Danaus, and the latter hated them and eventually somehow killed them and threw their heads or bodies into the marsh and so made it fruitful. And Danaus quickly procured other husbands for them by offering them, without bride-price, as prizes in a foot-race![1]

All this is fairly trivial; and it is not much helped by being tied up with the myth of Io. Danaus and his daughters are really descended from her, and when they come from Egypt to Argos are really returning to their own country. It is hard to imagine a less promising material for any sort of serious fiction, to say nothing of a great tragedy. Yet a tragedy is what Aeschylus makes of it. The initial absurdity of the fifty sons and fifty daughters hardly troubles him: for the early tragic chorus regularly consisted of fifty, and at the time of the *Supplices* tragedy was still little more than a choral dance. His play becomes a

---

[1] Pindar, *Pyth.* ix. 112 ff., who treats the story jestingly.

Choral Dance of Woman pursued by Man; pursued by unloved and violent Man, and therefore determined to die rather than submit. There is no individual anywhere. It is just Woman against Man, Woman asserting her right to her own body, proclaiming that the violation of that right is one of the eternal and unpardonable wrongs, and at last defending her honour by killing the would-be ravisher. And how does Io come in? Chiefly to deepen the issue; to show that these women are not the first women who have had to face the same trial, nor will they be the last. The Danaids only 'wander in the print of ancient feet'. Their ancestress Io was pursued in the same way by Zeus himself; generations of women have endured the same lot. This wrong is only part of the mystery of the world. The Danaids are ready for death rather than for submission, yet they know, and their handmaids warn them, that the odds are against them.

About Io and her problem there will be more to say in a later chapter; but, apart from Io, one may say that, in dealing with this childish piece of folk-lore, Aeschylus has selected one element only, brushing the rest aside, as he brushed aside the quarrel of Zeus and Prometheus about the burnt sacrifice, and in that one element has found or imagined one of the great fundamental problems of human life. That is *Semnotês*.

CHAPTER II

THE STAGE TECHNIQUE OF AESCHYLUS: EXPERIMENTS, *MECHANAI*, *TERATEIA*

THE classic stage of the fifth century settled down towards the end of the life of Aeschylus into a fairly uniform convention. *Skênographia*, which seems to mean 'scene painting', is said to have been introduced by Sophocles, but, if we understand the word aright, was certainly used in the last trilogy of Aeschylus. The back wall of the stage, which was at the same time the front wall of the booth (σκηνή) in which the actors dressed, was made to represent the front of a dwelling-place—palace or temple or hut—with a large door in the middle and two smaller doors at the sides. On each side of this front there were arrangements called περίακτοι or revolving doors, indicating the kind of scene—city, sea, or mountains—in which it stood. In later times the palace front might be decorated, as Vitruvius says, with columns, pediments, and statues, to give it an air of richness and dignity, and it had usually some form of gallery or upper story: but there was little or no attempt at what we call scenic effect. The background was merely a background; the effect of the drama was left to the actors and the words they spoke. One may compare the stage of Racine and Corneille, and that

which was usual in England and France in the
eighteenth century. The Greek drama in its
middle period was content with a severe *sôphrosynê*
or temperance in the use of scenery, and did not
rely on the stage carpenter for effects of romance
or terror. It also eschewed the use of μηχαναί,
or 'machines'; and when Euripides in his more
romantic plays reintroduced them, the Comic
writers immediately made them a subject for jokes.

What is not often realized is that, before settling
down to this discreet form, tragedy had made
much more ambitious experiments. Aeschylus
used *mêchanai* with much greater boldness than
Euripides. In his *Psychostasia*, or *Soul-Weighing*,
for instance, he showed Zeus in heaven weighing
the lives or fates of Memnon and Achilles, while
the mothers of the two heroes, Eôs and Thetis,
floated in air beside the balance; later on in the
same play Eôs descended from a kind of crane
and carried off the body of Memnon. But let us
look in detail at the scenic devices that are implied
in the *Prometheus*.

In the first place, there is a definite attempt at
producing by means of the scenery an effect of
romantic terror. Prometheus is bound to a wild
rock at the end of the world; it is a 'towering
precipice'. It is above a 'tempest-riven gulf'. And,
in the language of the stage, the rock is 'practi-
cable'; that is to say, it is really there, and when it
is hurled by lightning into the abyss it really goes.

There seems to have been just sufficient room for this in the old theatre of Dionysus. The gigantic figure of the Titan is crucified against the rock. How was this done?

It seems probable, in spite of the objections raised by Mazon and others,[1] that the object nailed upon the rock was a wooden structure and not a man. It was motionless: 'Upright, not closing eye nor bending knee' (l. 32). It was gigantic. When Hephaistos has fixed a bond round its chest, Kratos bids him 'Climb down', or at any rate 'Go down' (χώρει κάτω), in order to put the fetters round its ankles (74). It was fixed in a way not suited for a human being. A wedge of 'biting adamant' is driven right through its breast to pin it to the rock (65). Nails, or piercing gyves, are driven with a hammer through its feet (76). And one may notice that the magnificent silence of Prometheus during the scene while his tormentors are present, and his still more magnificent burst into speech when left alone (88), seem on this hypothesis to be nicely suited to stage conveniences. There are only two actors. They represent Hephaistos and Kratos—the other daemon does not speak—who nail the victim to the rock and depart; then one actor comes into the wooden figure and speaks for Prometheus.

A towering crag over a gulf, and a gigantic figure crucified against it: that is the permanent

---

[1] Mazon, *Eschyle*, i. 151.

scene. Next, there is a lavish use of *mêchanai*.
The Chorus of the Daughters of Ocean enter
flying; their approach is heralded by a sound of
great wings in the air; Prometheus is filled with
fear at the sound, doubtless because it suggests the
eagle which he knows will sooner or later come
to prey upon him. Then the Oceanides enter
through the air on a winged car (125–35).

At what level must we suppose them to enter?
They converse freely with Prometheus, and therefore must probably be nearer to his head than his
feet. Furthermore, at the end of the play, when
in return for his defiance Prometheus is hurled,
crag and all, down to the abyss, they are warned
to stand clear lest the lightning strike them or the
roar of the thunder drive them mad (1061). Their
answer is to defy the tortures, and casting away
all thoughts of safety, cling to him whom they
love (1017–20). The thunderbolt strikes, and
they sink with Prometheus to the deep. Therefore
presumably they were actually on the crag with
him. Thus they certainly enter at a high level;
and if they alight, must alight on the crag; they
are on the crag when it is cast into Hades: whether
in the meantime they go down to their normal
place in the orchestra or no it does not at first sight
seem possible to decide.

But let us look closer: at line 274 Prometheus
bids them 'alight on the ground' (πέδοι δὲ βᾶσαι),
and at lines 281 ff., after some conversation with

Prometheus, they announce that they are going
to leave the winged car and 'the air where the
great birds pass' and set foot upon 'this rocky
land'. Immediately afterwards their father Okeanos himself enters. He, like his daughters, enters
through the air, being mounted in fact on a flying
griffin, and there is no reason to suppose that he
ever descends from it during his short scene. But
the curious thing is that, though his daughters are
there, he says no word to them nor they to him,
and there is no sign that they see each other. The
thought suggests itself that perhaps the winged
car and the flying griffin balanced one another
at opposite ends of a double crane, and that as
Okeanos was swung on to the stage his daughters
by mechanical necessity were swung off. However, when Okeanos departs, we find them somewhere stationary, singing their first Stasimon
(399). One would suppose that they had come
down to *terra firma*, that is, to the orchestra below
the rock, where the Chorus normally belongs.
Perhaps, as Wilamowitz thinks, there is some conclusion to be drawn from the fact that at line 436,
after the first Stasimon, Prometheus apologizes for
his silence (436–8).

> Think not from pride, nor yet from bitterness
> I am silent.[1]

There has evidently been some pause during

---

[1] μήτοι χλιδῇ δοκεῖτε μηδ' αὐθαδίᾳ
σιγᾶν με.

which he might have been expected to speak. Conceivably it was caused by the necessity of bringing the Chorus from the place where the *mêchanê* had left them to the new position they were to occupy.

Two other characters make entrances and exits during the play. Is there any way of settling at what level they enter, whether up on the rock near the head of the giant figure, or down on the level ground of the orchestra? The first is Io, the victim of Zeus. She enters, mad, stung by the gad-fly, haunted by the ghost of the watcher Argos, whose eyes are stars. She is dancing, and she says in so many words that she is 'driven along the sand of the sea-shore' (573). Clearly, therefore, she enters on the level ground, not through the air, and performs her dance on the proper dancing-floor or orchestra. Yet later on, in the course of her conversation with Prometheus, she seems to have mounted the rock, for at line 747 she breaks out: 'Why should I live? Why do I not cast myself down from this rugged rock, to be dashed to the ground and be rid of my sorrows?' It is possible of course that she means 'Why do I not climb to the top of this rugged rock and then cast myself down', but the words would more naturally suggest that she is on the rock already.

The second is Hermes. When Hermes comes in the last scene to warn Prometheus and then let loose the thunderbolts upon him, there is no state-

ment made as to how he comes. However, it
seems fairly clear that he comes through the air
upon a *mêchanê*. We know that the *mêchanê* is
there, ready for use; Hermes is characteristically
a flying god, with wings upon his feet; and lastly
when the storm is about to be let loose Hermes
warns the Oceanides to move away from the
danger. Presumably he moves away himself; and
if so, surely the easiest and most effective method
of withdrawal is to sweep away through the air
by which he came.

I know of no other Greek play which at all
approaches the *Prometheus* in this ambitious and
romantic use of stage devices. The Greek word
for it is *terateia* (τερατεία), an untranslatable term
derived from τέρας, a 'marvel' or 'portent'. It is
a style which makes a constant appeal to the
sense of the marvellous. We may note that when
Aristotle seeks instances of *terateia*, he cites 'the
Phorkides and *Prometheus* and those that take
place in Hades'.[1] The gigantic figure, the flying car, the griffin, the hornèd Moon-maiden,
the storm, and the thunder-riven rock that sinks
into the abyss, make up a great sum total of
'marvellousness'.

[1] Ar. *Poet.* 1456ᵃ, τὸ Δὲ τερατῶΔες, οἶον αἵ τε ΦορκίΔες καὶ Προμηθεὺς καὶ ὅσα ἐν 'ΑίΔου. So most editors; Bywater prefers τὸ Δὲ τέταρ-
τον ὄψις (the fourth element is spectacle), which is nearer the MS.
but not so suitable in sense. Cf. the ancient *Life* of Aeschylus, ταῖς τε
γὰρ ὄψεσι καὶ τοῖς μύθοις πρὸς ἔκπληξιν τερατώΔη μᾶλλον ἢ πρὸς ἀπά-
την κέχρηται.

Tὸ τερατῶᾶες is Aristotle's phrase: ἔκπληξις τερα-
τώᾶης ('a marvelling amazement') is the phrase
specially used in the ancient *Life* of Aeschylus,
when explaining that he aimed at producing this
effect rather than realistic 'illusion' (ἀπάτη). We
have no other example of this style in our remains
of Greek tragedy; and I cannot help connecting
with it the equally unexampled treatment of the
lyrics and the dancing. Westphal in 1868 pointed
out the peculiarities of the *Prometheus* in this respect: the monodies of Prometheus and of Io; the
brevity of the actual Choral songs; and the amazing
arrangement by which the Chorus remains either
flying on a machine or stationary on a crag, while
the real dancing is done by a single figure, Io.
Westphal argued rightly that such treatment of
the Chorus was utterly unlike what we find in the
rest of Aeschylus; so it is. But it is equally unlike
Sophocles and Euripides and every remnant of
Greek drama that we possess, and nothing is
gained by calling it 'post-Aeschylean', or arguing,
with Bethe, that it must be later than the inven-
tions of 420 B.C. The peculiarity is not a matter
of date. It must, I think, be a matter of style; it
must be that the 'marvellous style' (τὸ τερατῶᾶες
εἶᾶος) added to its effects of abnormality by an
abnormal treatment of the dances and consequently of the lyrics. The language of the *Prometheus* lyrics is quite markedly Aeschylean; no
one that we know of after 456 B.C. ever wrote

again like that.[1] The metres have nothing very peculiar about them except, perhaps, the curious sequence of different metres in Prometheus' monologue 93–128. There we have first iambics 88–92, then anapaests 93–100, then iambics again 101–13; then lyrical iambics 114–19, then anapaests again. And one must remember that the figure of Prometheus is stationary all the time. The changes are very curious, and must have some dramatic purpose. I would suggest that they are meant to convey the effect of a series of long solitary periods of waiting better than could be done in a single continuous speech. But, however that may be, I think we are safe in saying that this unexampled treatment of the Chorus and the lyrics, occurring in the play which is our only example of the 'marvellous style', is most naturally to be regarded as a mark of that style.

To return to the *mêchanai* as the most obvious instruments of *terateia*, we may notice that Aeschylus tried something of the same sort in one or two of the lost plays. In the *Psychostasia*, or Memnon-trilogy, there were *mêchanai* carrying at least three gods and two souls.[2] In the *Perseus* trilogy that hero entered flying through the air. In the *Europa* or *Kares* the brothers Sleep and

---

[1] e.g. (547) οὐδ' ἐλέρχθης ὀλιγοδρανίαν ἄκικυν ἰσόνειρον . . . or (898) ταρβῶ γὰρ ἀστεργάνορα παρθενίαν εἰσορῶσ' Ἰοῦς ἀμαλαπτομέναν δυσπλάνοις Ἥρας ἀλατείαις πόνων.

[2] See above, p. 38, and cf. the *Life*, § 14.

Death flew down to carry the dead body of Sarpêdon back to his home in Lycia. After that the use of *mêchanai* seems to have gone out. There is nothing unusual in this. It often happens that a more critical age rejects the crude ingenuities which have dazzled its predecessor. The Elizabethans did not, I think, use in serious drama the angels suspended from the roof which were used and doubtless admired in medieval liturgical plays. The stage of Dryden would not admit heroes riding on Elizabethan hobby-horses. The rather fascinating phenomenon called 'Pepper's ghost', produced by having a real figure below the stage reflected in a large sheet of plain glass on the stage, suspended at the proper angle, had a great success when first introduced, but was quickly dropped in the next generation and is almost unknown to modern actors. I suspect, therefore, that the ambitious *mêchanai* and masks of Aeschylus seemed crude and unsatisfying to an age which had a higher standard of stage illusion. Euripides revived the aerial *mêchanê* for his gods who spoke judgement from on high at the very end of the play, where the dramatic illusion was already beginning to melt away into mere narrative or prophecy. He tried it in his *Bellerophon* in the actual body of the play, but the experiment was mocked at and parodied in comedy. It was perhaps a romantic archaism when he brought Perseus through the air on wings in his *Andromeda*, but the case was a special one, since it was an essential datum of the tradition that Perseus had magic wings. He could scarcely have appeared without them.

Doubtless if the machinery at the disposal of a fifth-century stage carpenter had been very much better than it was, this effort after 'the marvellous' would have been carried farther. It is perhaps fortunate that, in its resolute *Sophrosynê*, Greek tragedy gave up the effects which it had not the means of bringing off successfully, and concentrated on the more inward elements of drama. But it is interesting to note how Aeschylus did strive in imagination after effects which he could not reach; like Shakespeare in *King Lear*, like Ibsen in *John Gabriel Borkman*, both of which plays demand of the stage carpenter far more than he can give them in the way of storms and mountain avalanches and *terateia* in general. But there is also a curious contrast. Shakespeare and Ibsen demanded more and more of their instrument as they grew older, and eventually strained it to breaking-point. I think the same might be said of many great modern writers. It is surely characteristic of the Greek genius that Aeschylus began by making extravagant demands on scene and language and then deliberately reduced them; that Euripides wrote a first version of the *Hippolytus* full of strong theatrical effects and then in an improved second version deliberately threw them away;[1] that the early epic poetry was, to judge by all the evidence, full of marvels and bloody horrors, which have been systematically suppressed in our *Iliad*. In each case the poet ultimately attains his end not by *Sturm und Drang* but by an inspired *Sôphrosynê*.

It was not only in the *Prometheus* that Aeschylus took a line which was not followed by the conventions of classical tragedy. The *Supplices*, or *Suppliant Women*, is not an example of 'the marvellous', but it is the earliest, and in my judgement far the earliest, Greek play that has come down to us, and is therefore extraordinarily interesting

---

[1] ἐμφαίνεται Δὲ ὕστερος γεγραμμένος, τὸ γὰρ ἀπρεπὲς καὶ κακηγορίας ἄξιον ἐν τούτωι Διώρθωται τῶι Δράματι, says Aristophanes of Byzantium. It is a well-established rule that a later version of any phrase or tale 'goes one better' than its predecessors. To give one clear case, quoted by Conington: Homer (*Il.* B. 488) says he could not tell all the Greek forces if he had ten tongues (οὐΔ' εἴ μοι Δέκα μὲν γλῶσσαι, Δέκα Δὲ στόματ' ἦσαν). Vergil in a similar situation requires a hundred: 'non mihi si linguae centum sint, guttura centum.' Statius, if I remember rightly, somewhere requires a thousand. At any rate Pope, in translating, makes Homer's ten into a thousand, Ogilby having already made them into a hundred. Consequently, it is surprising to find that, according to all the evidence, the version of the *Hippolytus* which has come down to us, being the second and improved version, is decidedly less sensational than the earlier play, which we chiefly know from various allusions and from Seneca's imitation. For instance, in the earlier version Phaedra pleads with Hippolytus for his love, and justifies herself by Theseus' infidelities. I suspect that Euripides was using as his source a story like the story of Joseph, or of the Egyptian *Two Brothers*, and began by simply putting the events of the story on the stage. Then, on reflection, he saw that the stage required a different treatment. As to the 'expurgation' of the epic, opinions differ, but see my *Rise of the Greek Epic*, edn. 4, pp. 126 ff.

to the archaeologist. We know that tragedy arose from the dithyramb, that is from one form of the simple communal dance upon a circular dancing-ground or threshing-floor. We know that the Chorus consisted originally of fifty persons, and finally of twelve; and it seems likely that this came about by dividing the fifty persons among the four plays of the tetralogy, making twelve each and two over. These two would give us the two actors, or, if the poet himself took part, the three actors. Now in the *Supplices* the Chorus consists of the fifty daughters of Danaus and therefore numbers fifty. It must date from the time before the original Chorus was broken up. But that is by no means all. The fifty Danaids are pursued by the fifty sons of Aegyptus, or rather by an army of Egyptian slaves representing them and led by a Herald. I think it is clear that these slaves numbered at least fifty also, since, when they appear, the Danaids, though courageous and even Amazonian in character, fly in terror and never think of resisting them. Furthermore, the fifty Egyptians are put to flight in turn by the Argive army, which must, therefore, at a modest estimate, be reckoned at least at another fifty. That gives us a hundred and fifty persons present on the dancing-floor at once, without counting the 'Exarchontes' or Directors of the three Choruses. For the Danaids are directed by their father, Danaus; the Argive Army is directed by the King, and the Egyptian

horde by a Herald. There are no other characters;
that is to say, there are in the strict sense of the
word no independent actors at all: only three
Choruses, each fifty strong, each with its Director,
or Exarchon. This Exarchon, as I have explained
elsewhere, is distinct from the ordinary Cory-
phaeus or leader of the Chorus. The Danaids are
led by the First Danaid, but directed by Danaus;
the Egyptians are led by the First Egyptian, but
directed by the Herald, and so on ; just as in the
Bacchae, for example, the Chorus of Maenads is
led by the First Maenad, but directed by Dionysus; in the *Ichneutae* the Chorus of Satyrs is led
by the First Satyr but directed by the Father of
the Satyrs, Silenus.

Thus we have no actors, no stage, but at least
a hundred and fifty-three persons engaged in a
complex of dances on the old dancing-floor of
Dionysus. It is interesting to note that in the
Theatre of Dionysus at Athens the old dancing-
floor was a good deal larger than the orchestra of
the classical theatre; it was a complete circle, 24
metres, or over 26 yards, in diameter. That would
give moving space to a good many more than a
hundred and fifty persons. And it is just possible
that all the figures we have used ought to be
doubled. For at the end of the play we find that
each of the Danaids had with her a Handmaid,
and the Handmaids form into another Chorus.
That makes a hundred Danaids and Handmaids

together; to frighten whom it would presumably
take a hundred Egyptians, who again would
hardly give up all fight before less than a hundred
Argives. However, there is no earlier trace of the
Handmaids' presence. I suspect that they were
only introduced in the last scene, when the performers who represented the Egyptians had just
made their exit a few minutes before and were
therefore available as a new Chorus in a new dress.

Practically no scenery; a large round dancing-
place and great masses of performers in rich and
varied costume: the production would be rather
like those with which Reinhardt made such an
impression at the beginning of this century, mass-
ing his hundreds of performers in some circus or
stadium or the vast enclosure at Olympia. Aeschylus did not neglect what Aristotle calls the
element of ὄψις, or spectacle, but he obtained it
in this case through mass, dance, and costume.
We know from the *Frogs* that he was conspicuous
for his use of gorgeous costumes, and he seems
especially to have been so in the *Supplices*. The
Suppliants themselves form strange exotic figures.
Their cheeks are dark and glowing; they have Ty-
rian veils; the Argive King seeing them asks (235)

> What company in all un-Greek array,
> Rich with barbarian robes and coifing gay,
> Awaits us here? For, sure, not Argolis,
> Not Hellas, knows such woman's garb as this.

Afterwards (285) he compares them to Amazons, and before that to Libyan women, or Egyptian, or Cyprian, or to those Indian women who

roam

> By camels drawn, each in her tented home,
> Beyond the wallèd Ethiop, in waste lands.

The Egyptian slaves again, described by Wilamowitz as a 'mob of black and yellow devils', must have had a striking appearance. We hear of their black limbs showing against their robes of white (719); we hear of their loud threats and jeers; they crawl (896) like asps, they dart like black spiders (888). And we can hardly suppose that the chivalrous Argive soldiers were allowed to present a less impressive appearance. Then, more fortunate than Reinhardt, Aeschylus had to his hand a people accustomed to express their feelings by complicated and highly emotional dancing. Three of the dances in particular strike one as interesting and picturesque, though of course we cannot conjecture with any approach to certainty what the steps or movements were. There is a long dance at the beginning where the fugitive maidens meditate on the strange sufferings of their ancestress, the hornèd Io, and 'wander in the print of ancient feet'; there is an impassioned dance of flight and pursuit, at the end of which the black persecutors drag the maidens by their hair from the altar; and there is a delightful water-charm and prayer for fruitfulness at the end.[1] The general effect is

---

[1] 40 ff., 825 ff., 1018 ff.

curiously different from that of the *Prometheus*:
here masses of performers, rich costumes, long and
thrilling dances, no stage machines and no scenery:
in the *Prometheus* no masses, no stress on costume,
one dance by a single dancer, Io; but machines
and scenery of the most daring inventiveness.
Both plays depart widely from the limits afterwards imposed by ordinary fifth-century convention.

We must now make one correction in this account of the setting of the *Supplices*. We spoke of
it as being a plain circular dancing-ground, or
Orchestra, with no stage, and in a sense this is true;
but if there was no stage proper, there was a high
place of some sort on which a performer could stand
and see over the heads of the rest. It is several times
called a 'hill', πάγος (189). It is also a 'place of
watch', σκοπή (713). It is also, or at least it contains,
a κοινοβωμία (222) or collection of altars to the
various Gods of the Assembly or Gathering. It
is large enough to give standing-room to the fifty
Danaids with their father, and possibly to the fifty
Danaids and the fifty persecutors at once. When
space is needed in the dancing-ground for the
entrance or manœuvring of any large body of
performers, those present seem always to retire on
to this high place. For instance, at line 208,

I fain would make my seat beside thine own,

the Danaids join their father among the altars;
that leaves room for the entrance of the King and

the Argive Army. At line 825, the Danaids either
fly towards the high place or try to escape from
the orchestra as the Egyptians enter; at 911, both
Egyptians and Danaids seem to be up among the
altars when the Argive soldiers enter again.

How are we to conceive this Hill or High Place?
In particular, was it a real hill built up in the
centre of the Orchestra, where in later tragedy the
central altar regularly stood, or was it a long rectangular erection at the back, where in later tragedy
there was a stage? It is hard to say with certainty,
since both possibilities seem to occur in other
plays.

In the *Prometheus* there is the high rock on
which the giant is nailed; that must have been at
the back of the scene. To put it in the centre
would produce intolerable difficulties.

In the *Seven against Thebes* there is a citadel
with altars: during the siege the frightened women
fly thither for refuge, partly because the citadel
is the strongest point, partly from a wish to kneel
at the altars. This must be at the back of the
scene; a citadel erected in the centre would be
impossible. It would look too tiny; also the audience would see round it, and consequently would
expect to see some of the seven gates and the seven
armies attacking.

We may also notice that, in both the *Supplices*
and the *Seven against Thebes* (110–80), there is on
the High Place a *Koinobomia*, and, as far as I know,

all the *Koinobomiae* which are represented in our remains of ancient art are long rectangular structures, suitable for the back of a scene, not for the centre.

In the *Persae* the arrangement seems to be different. There is an ὄχθος (647), or 'mound', which is the Tomb of Darius, and from which his Ghost rises. There is also a στέγος ἀρχαῖον (141), an 'ancient building', on the steps of which the elders sit, and which seems to represent the Council Chamber. Wilamowitz considers that there was only one erection, which served first for a Council Chamber and then for the King's Tomb, and that it formed the back of the scene. But it works better to suppose that we have in the *Persae* the regular conventional scene; at the back a palace front with steps before it, which in the first scene represents the Elders' Council Chamber and later the Palace of Atossa; and in the centre of the orchestra a raised altar or tomb—the two were often indistinguishable—out of which the Ghost rises. This is exactly the arrangement used afterwards in the *Choëphoroe*; a Palace Front at the back, to be used when the action takes place at the palace, and a tomb or altar in the centre, to be used when the scene is at Agamemnon's tomb.

On the whole, therefore, it looks as if the setting of the *Supplices* was simply the large round dancing floor with the wall of the actor's dressing-room at the back so treated as to look like a High

Place, with a broad flight of wooden steps leading up to it and a row of altars along the ridge.

Let us turn to a subject now on which much, perhaps too much, has already been written, the diction of Aeschylus. It is of course impossible to convey any adequate idea of his style, its majesty, its beauty or its strangeness, except by a minute and loving study of his actual text. But the particular points about it which need emphasizing here can, I think, be made clear by mere description.

We all know that the characteristic of Attic prose style was something which the ancient critics called λιτότης, 'plainness' or 'simplicity'. The Attic of Lysias or Demosthenes as contrasted with the Ionic style of Herodotus or the Sicilian of Gorgias was a little like the English style of Addison or Dryden as contrasted with that of Hooker or Milton. It was like the early eighteenth century as opposed to the seventeenth. It aimed at clarity of thought and expression: it rejected the fantastic, the pretentious, the obscure. It rejected exaggerated sentiments and strange exotic words. The taste of his time is well summed up by Aristotle (*Rhet*. iii. 1. 9):

'Since poets seemed to win fame through their fine language when their thoughts were simple enough, the language of oratorical prose at first took a poetical colour, e.g. that of Gorgias. Even now most uneducated people think that poetical language makes the finest writing. This is a mistake. The language of prose is distinct from that of poetry, a point which is made clearer by what takes place on the stage to-day, when even the language of tragedy has altered its character. Just as iambics were adopted instead of tetrameters because they are the most prose-like of all metres, so tragedy has given up all those words not used in ordinary talk which decorated the early drama and are still used by writers of hexameter poems. It is therefore ridiculous to imitate a poetical manner which the poets themselves have dropped.'

A touch of the Philistine does sometimes show itself in Aristotle. But, though he is writing at a later period, the tendency which he observed began to rise quite early in the history of tragedy. The dialogue especially aims more and more at λιτότης and σαφήνεια, 'plainness' and 'lucidity'. Tragedy becomes possessed by that form of the classical spirit which consists in self-restraint and *sôphrosynê*. This often disappoints our modern taste. Many scholars who love the poetry of Homer, Theocritus, and the Anthology are rather repelled by the classic severity of the Attic drama; it seems to them not to read like real poetry.

Now here again Aeschylus is pre-classical. He can of course, when he chooses, use with tremendous effect the simplest possible language: Clytemnestra's statement

οὗτός ἐστιν Ἀγαμέμνων, ἐμὸς πόσις

could hardly be simpler: nor could the last terrible
words of the fury-haunted Orestes:

ὑμεῖς μὲν οὐχ ὁρᾶτε τάσδ', ἐγὼ δ' ὁρῶ.

But such lines are all the more striking because
in general Aeschylus revels, like any romantic, in
effects of language. He likes his poetry gorgeous
and thrilling, and does not bother about such dull
things as self-restraint. This characteristic lies at
the back of the contest between him and Euripides
in the *Frogs*, where Euripides, in the true Attic
style of ῥητορική—almost the opposite of what we
call 'rhetoric'—insists on clearness, correctness,
simplicity, and the complete rejection of bom-
bast; Aeschylus knows nothing of this artificial
severity, and insists that if heroes and demi-
gods are to speak, and to speak in moments of
passion, they must use a language far more
majestic than that of common life. In the *Frogs*
he argues that the poet has a civic or moral function (1054):

AESCHYLUS

. . . It's his duty to teach, and you know it.
As a child learns from all who may come in his way, so
the grown world learns from a poet.
Oh, words of good counsel should flow from his
voice. . . .

EURIPIDES

And words like Mount Lycabettus
Or Parnês, such as you give us for choice, must needs
be good counsel? Oh, let us,
Oh, let us at least speak the language of men!

AESCHYLUS

Flat cavil, Sir! Cavil absurd,
When the subject is great and the sentiment, then, of
necessity, great grows the word.
When heroes give range to their thoughts, is it strange
if the speech of them over us towers?
Why, the garb of them too should be gorgeous to view,
and majestical, nothing like ours!
All this I saw and established as law, till you came and
spoilt it.

A little later (1068) he makes his last general
charge against the atmosphere of Euripides' poetry:
it was too dependent on *rhetorikê*, which, we must
remember, implied a theory of style which carefully avoided poetical language:

Then next you have trained in the speech-making arts
nigh every infant that crawls.
Oh, this is the thing that such havoc has wrought in
the wrestling-school; narrowed the hips
Of the poor, pale, chattering children, and taught the
crews of the pick of the ships
To answer back pat to their officer's nose! How unlike
my old sailor of yore,
With no thought in his head but to guzzle his brose,
and sing as he bent at the oar!

No doubt Aeschylus' old sailors, like Aristotle's
'uneducated man', enjoyed poetical language and
did not understand the sneers of the high-
brows.

There is a note of the Scholiast on a certain
passage of the *Choëphoroe* (425–9), saying κωμω-
λεῖται ὡς Διθυραμβῶλες, 'This is ridiculed as

dithyrambic'.[1] The dithyrambic style was that ultra-poetical semi-nonsensical style used, for example, by the poets who are brought on the stage in Aristophanes, full of strange compound words about snow and wings and clouds and love and ecstasy.[2] The passage in the *Choëphoroe* passes my wit to translate, but I may observe that it has close-packed together the exotic word (γλῶσσα) ἰηλεμίστρια, a dirge-woman, and the otherwise unknown adjectives ἀπρικτόπληκτα, meaning 'smiting and at the same time tearing', πολυπάλακτα 'much-besprinkled', ἐπασσυτεροτριβῆ 'one-on-top-of-another-rubbing', all applied to the motion of the hands of the mourner. In the first Chorus of the *Choëphoroe* we have the magnificent phrase ἀωρό-νυκτον ἀμβόαμα, meaning 'a cry in the dead of night'. In the *Supplices* a woman wishes to throw herself over a precipice which she describes by six continuous adjectives 'a smooth goat-deserted,

---

[1] *Cho.* 425–9

> ἔκοψα κομμὸν Ἄριον ἔν τε Κισσίας
> νόμοις ἰηλεμιστρίας,
> ἀπρικτόπληκτα πολυπάλακτα δ' ἦν ἰδεῖν
> ἐπασσυτεροτριβῆ τὰ χερὸς ὀρέγματα,
> ἄνωθεν ἀνέκαθεν, κτύπωι δ' ἐπερρόθει
> κροτητὸν ἀμὸν καὶ πανάθλιον κάρα.

(With the dirge of Agbatana I beat my breast,
　　Like the keeners of Kissia I make songs of pain;
Lo, yearnings of arms abundant, east and west;
　　Tearing they smite, again and yet again,
From above, from high: yea, God hath smitten red
This bitter bleeding bosom, this bended head.)

[2] Cf. *Birds*, ll. 1387 ff.

undeciphered, lonely-brooding, pendant vulture's
crag'.[1] In the *Prometheus* (547 f.) the daughters
of Ocean ask what the hero could ever hope to
gain from man: 'Sawest thou not the little-doing,
strengthless, dreamlike, wherein the blind race of
mortals is prisoned', where practically every word
in the Greek is a strange poetical word. These
passages are exceedingly beautiful, but it is a kind
of beauty against which the classical spirit in drama
generally tried to set its face, even in lyrics. Aeschylus uses it freely in lyrics, and occasionally
even in dialogue, when he speaks of great subjects
as in the leaping and untranslatable lines in the
Persae (811 ff.) about the destruction of altars and
shrines

βωμοὶ Δ' ἄιστοι Δαιμόνων θ' ἱΔρύματα
πρόρριζα φύρΔην ἐξανέστραπται βάθρων.

He is also capable of a grandiloquent phrase to
describe things not to our minds particularly impressive, like the beard of one of the slain Persian
satraps, πυρσὴν ʒαπληθῆ Δάσκιον γενειάΔα (316)
'red, abounding, deep-shadowed'—and now
stained a deeper red.

There is another peculiarity of diction, characteristic of much primitive poetry, which classical
tragedy seems to have considered childish and
eschewed: I mean the use of riddling phrases or
what in Icelandic literature are called 'kennings'.

[1] (794 f.) λισσὰς αἰγίλιψ ἀπρόσΔεικτος οἰόφρων κρεμὰς
γυπιὰς πέτρα.

Instead of the sea you say 'the swan-bath', instead of fire 'the red cock', instead of ships, 'the black dragons'. Homer uses such 'kennings' for describing various gods and goddesses: 'the renowned lame one', περικλυτὸς ἀμφιγυήεις, for Hephaistos; 'the rosy-fingered early-born', ῥοδοδάκτυλος ἠρι-γένεια, for Dawn; 'the Earth-shaker', Ἐννοσίγαιος, for Poseidon; and many phrases of which the meaning was already lost in the fifth century, such as Διάκτορος Ἀργεϊφόντης for Hermes, καλὴ ἁλοσύδνη for the Sea-goddess. Hesiod abounds in kennings of a more familiar sort, such as 'House-carrier' for snail, 'Boneless' for the octopus, 'Clever' for the ant.[1] Aeschylus in the exuberance of his joy in language uses kennings a good deal. The fish that devour the Persian dead at Salamis are ἄναυδοι παῖδες τᾶς ἀμιάντου, 'voiceless children of the undefiled' (*Pers.* 577). But he generally makes a compromise with the Attic demand for lucidity by adding the interpretation afterwards, a practice which the Hesiodic poets or the early Norsemen would have considered hardly playing the game. He speaks of 'Jove's winged hound, the red eagle' (*Prom.* 1022); 'the flower-worker's distillation, bright honey' (*Pers.* 612). So ships are 'they of

---

[1] φερέοικος *Op.* 571, ἀνόστεος ib. 524, ἴδρις ib. 778. Homer uses ὑγρη 'the wet' for the sea and τραφερήν τε καὶ ὑγρὴν for land and sea. These cases seem to be different from the riddle-names applied by hunters to various beasts in order that the beasts may not know that they are being talked about (e.g. the Arabs, 'Lord Johan-ben-el-Johan' for the lion). See Sinclair on *Op.* 524.

the flaxen wings, of the dark blue eyes', but the word
'ships' is immediately added (*Pers.* 559). Sometimes the interpretation comes first, and the ken-
ning becomes a mere epithet: 'smoke, the colour-
shot sister of fire', 'dust, the voiceless herald of an
army'. 'Dust' in another place is 'the thirsty sister
of mud',[1] but there, I think, the grotesque phrase
has a special meaning. A Herald is seen who is,
for dramatic purposes, supposed to have come
straight from the battle-field without changing his
clothes, and the mire of battle has caked into dust
upon his garments. Our generation has seen many
such arrivals at Victoria or Waterloo. Readers
have puzzled much over the διπλῆ μάστιγι τὴν
Ἄρης φιλεῖ in *Ag.* 643, though he proceeds to
explain it

> The twofold scourge that sateth Ares' lust,
> Spear crossed with spear, dust wed with bloody dust.

Another daring experiment would seem at first
blush to be doomed to certain failure, yet Aeschylus makes of it an indubitable success. It is the
attempt to get the requisite foreign or exotic
atmosphere in the scenes where the characters are
Persian, Egyptian, or Ionian, by making them use
an exotic diction. They speak Greek, of course;
there is no doubt about that; but by means of
strange words, strange exclamations, and unusual
effects of metre, Aeschylus makes their Greek

---

[1] *Theb.* 494; *Suppl.* 180; *Ag.* 495.

sound as if it was foreign. In the *Persae* when the
Persian Elders are evoking the dead King Darius
from his grave, this is very marked (647–51),
657–80). The effect of course is cumulative;
there are strange ejaculations, οἶ and ἠὲ as well as
αἰαῖ; instead of the ordinary form ἄνακτα Δαρεῖον
they invoke θεῖον ἀνάκτορα Δαριᾶνα, Δαριὰν being
merely a by-form of the name Darius. Then
comes a word βαλήν or βαλλήν, said to be an
Asiatic word for Lord or Master, and perhaps
really a representation of some Semitic form like
'Ba'alênu'—that is, 'Ba'al' with the possessive suffix
of the first person plural, 'Our Ba'al'—and then a
hiatus ἴθι, ἱκοῦ, very strange in Greek poetry.[1] The
effect is absolutely that of strange oriental beings
speaking a strange oriental language, an effect confirmed by the last line βάσκε, πάτερ ἄκακε, Δαριὰν,
οἶ. It means merely 'Come, O father untouched
by evil, Darius, Oh!' But the word for 'come' is
Homeric and rare; the word 'untouched by evil' is
as odd in Greek as 'unevil' would be in English;
Darius is called 'Dariân', and the exclamation at
the end is *Oi*. At the end of the same chorus comes
a phrase 'ships that are no ships,' νᾶες ἄναες. It
is quite good intelligible Greek, yet as it comes
with one repetition, νᾶες ἄναες ἄναες, it sounds
like an inarticulate lament. There is a reference

---

[1] Βαλλήν, ἀρχαῖος βαλλήν, ἴθι, ἱκοῦ. The word occurs in various
scholia and lexica. It is Phrygian, according to Hesych. and Sext.
Emp.; Lycian or even Thurian (?) according to others.

to this outlandishness of language in a verse of
the *Frogs* (1028):

Why yes, when Darius arose from the grave, it gave me
　　genuine joy;
And the Chorus stood with its arms a-wave, and
　　observed 'Yow-oy, Yow-oy'.[1]

In the *Persae* this curious experiment seems to
me extraordinarily successful and moving. In
Aeschylus' earlier play, the *Supplices*, it seems to
have been made with less skill or tact, and with
disturbing results upon our manuscripts. The
Suppliant Women, Egyptian indeed but of true
Greek descent, are pursued by a hideous rabble
of negroid slaves from Egypt, led by a brutal
Herald. The effect is somewhat dream-like: the
virgin pursued by the ravisher, the white girl pursued by something black and dreadful, the Greek
woman—or, as we should say, the English woman
—pursued by a creature of foreign speech. The
Herald in our manuscripts talks sometimes an un-
intelligible gibberish. The text is almost certainly
corrupt, but the reason of the corruption probably
is that Aeschylus had gone so far in the direction
of barbarizing his speech that the scribes had failed
to understand it. You can just make out in the
confusion words that sound like 'blood', 'brand-
ing', 'beheading', 'force', and 'horror'. It is noteworthy that the speeches of the Danaids in the

---

[1] *Frogs* 1028 ὁ χορὸς δ' εὐθὺς τὼ χεῖρ' ὡδὶ συγκρούσας εἶπεν
Ἰαυοῖ.

same scene show no great degree of corruption
(825–92).

Tragedy never indulged in this sort of daring
after Aeschylus. The best instance we have of it
comes in a very curious document, discovered in
Egypt in the year 1902, and evidently based on
an imitation of Aeschylus. In the dithyramb
called *Persae* by the poet Timotheos, a famous, or
notorious, representative of the 'New Music' which
so troubled the end of the fifth century, we have
not only extremely dithyrambic language, we have
an actual imitation of a Persian comically praying for
mercy and talking broken ungrammatical Greek.[1]
The effect seems to me horrible. It is an example of
the kind of art that Plato particularly denounces,
the art that does not distinguish between good
and bad, appropriate or inappropriate, but aims at
making effects—just effects, of any and every kind.

Akin to this experiment is a much less daring
one: the representation on the tragic stage of common or uneducated persons. Shakespeare meets
the difficulty by sandwiching comic or prose
scenes in between his poetical or lofty scenes,
though even he seldom or never mixes the two

---

[1] Timotheos, *Persae*, 161 ff. The Persian speaks bad Greek, Ἰάονα
γλῶσσαν ἐξιχνεύων· Ἐγὼ μοί σοι, κῶς καὶ τί πρᾶγμα; αὖτις οὔλαμ'
ἔλθω . . . οὐκέτι μάχεσ' αὖτις ἐνθάδ' ἔρχω. Timotheos uses 'kennings'
in the same highly Baroque style: στόματος δ' ἐξάλλοντο μαρμαρο-
φεγγεῖς παῖδες συγκρουόμενοι, i.e. the man's teeth. I fear one must
admit that the Phrygian in Euripides' *Orestes* shows signs of the
beginnings of the Timothean style.

styles. Greek tragedy was, of course, in this respect more like Racine than Shakespeare, and
never admitted comic scenes in a tragedy. Aeschylus has one pathetic and half-comic character,
the Old Nurse of Orestes in the *Choëphoroe*, who
comes on in floods of tears at the news of Orestes'
death and talks in slightly ungrammatical language
about the mishaps of his babyhood (*Cho.* 734–65).
This particular effect is not repeated in the extant
specimens of Greek tragedy. In the *Antigone*,
indeed, Sophocles makes a poignant scene by
means of the psychology of the common soldier
who has been set to watch the corpse of Polynices.
He is terrified by Creon's anger when it appears
that some one has performed burial rites over
the body when he was not looking, and then
thoroughly pleased and happy when he discovers
the culprit and can offer Antigone to the execu-
tioner instead of himself. But the man's language
is in the tragic style, and his description of the
dust-storm particularly beautiful. In Euripides'
Theseus, we are told, there was a scene where a
slave who cannot read describes the marks upon
the sail of a ship which he has seen from a hill-top:
they are the letters ΘΗΣΕΥΣ. In the *Orestes*
there is a painful scene in which a terrified Phrygian slave begs mercy from the half-mad hero,
who plays with him like a cat with a mouse. But
the Phrygian, however contemptible in morale, is
quite grammatical and correct in his speech. Only

Aeschylus, still experimenting and creating, is unaffected by this Attic severity. It is only he who
makes Orestes, when the madness is coming upon
him, show signs of it in his broken sentences and
obscure diction as well as the wild splendour of
his eloquence (e.g. *Cho.* 269–98, 973–1043); only
he who represents a man so overcome with emotion
as to speak disjointedly and ungrammatically, like
the Herald in the *Agamemnon* (551–82).

Professor Baldensperger in his lectures on comparative literature has made an illuminating remark on the difference between the romantic and
the classical styles. The romantic is the earlier and
more natural; it is the unreformed unimprisoned
expression of the poetic impulse. Classicism is
a sort of Puritan reformation, rejecting what is
false or unreasonable, controlling what tends to
be unrestrained. It imposes a law of *Sôphrosynê*
upon the chaos of emotional or fanciful expression.
Its immense value to art can be estimated not
merely by setting against the *Iliad* the shapeless
exaggerations of Indian epics, and the vague-
ness of Irish legends, but still more perhaps
by trying to realize the innumerable cases where
the raw materials of poetry, in the form of story,
fancy, and emotion alike, have been present in
abundance, but, for lack of artistic firmness and
self-control, no poem has resulted. Still no doubt
classicism sometimes pays a heavy price for the
cosmos that it creates. In many ways Aeschylus

the creator of classical tragedy was himself still a romantic.

There is one further point in which Aeschylus makes the impression of a romantic. It is a technical point connected with his use of lyric metres. There is a curious heresy, which always obtains a few adherents among scholars of successive generations, that the *Prometheus* and perhaps also the *Supplices* are not really by Aeschylus. One of the arguments on which this view is sometimes based is his free and almost voluptuous treatment of the Ionic metres. Such treatment, it is argued, is soft, sophisticated, and obviously post-Euripidean; it cannot come in the early and severe stage of Attic tragedy. We know how sensitive the Greeks were to the moral and psychological implications of music; Plato and others are severe upon the unmanly and decadent character of the Ionian music as compared with the Dorian or even Phrygian. The Anacreontic verse is the obvious example; and we know that a loose form of Ionic metre was very common for love-poems in Alexandrian and even in Roman times.

The Ionic foot is of four syllables, two short followed by two long. It is written regularly as in Horace's:

Miserarum 'st I neque amori I dare ludum I neque dulci I
or in

ἔμε δείλαν, ἔμε παίσαν κακοτάτων πεδέχοισαν [1]

----

[1] Alcaeus A. 10 Lobel.

or with variations such as anaclasis, syncope, or
the like: for example, the Anacreontic:

σὺ δέ μ', ὦ μάκαιρα Δίρκα, στεφανηφόρους ἀπωθῇ
θιάσους ἔχουσαν ἔν σοι. τί μ' ἀναίνῃ; τί με φεύγεις;[1]

Now the mistake made, in my opinion, by these
critics, is to suppose that the gradual loosening of
music and metre, spoken of by Plato and Aristophanes, is the whole story. It clearly is not.
Anacreon was writing Ionic metres in Athens at
the court of Pisistratus, before the Attic dramatists
were born. The movement represented by Plato
and to a less extent by Aristophanes was part of
the Attic reformation: a pruning of the exuberance of Ionia, an insistence on severity, discipline,
and what may be called the Dorian side of life.
Aeschylus was writing before that movement began, and wrote naturally under the influence of
his predecessors, especially Phrynichus. Phrynichus, hopelessly outdistanced as a dramatist by
Aeschylus and his successors, was loved in Aristophanes' day for one thing: the sweetness of his old
Ionian songs. The old men, who as boys had
fought at Marathon, are described in a well-known
passage as going out to their business at dawn
humming Phrynichus' old lyrics; and we find, as
a matter of fact, that to a great extent they sing
in his Ionics (*Wasps* 281–315).

---

[1] Eur. *Bacch.* 530 ff.

Lamps in their hands, old music on their lips
Wild honey and the East and loveliness.[1]

It is surely natural enough that Aeschylus,
whenever his subjects deal with Ionia or the Greek
Orient, as in the *Persae* and the *Supplices*, should
use the Ionian metres in the same soft, sweet, style
that he had learnt from Phrynichus and even
Anacreon; I think it is natural also that when the
Daughters of Ocean, with all their Homeric
associations, come to weep with Prometheus at his
rock in the Far East, they also come through the
air with the same lovely Ionian music on their
wings. Here also Aeschylus is romantic; the
classic rules are not yet binding upon him.[2]

---

[1] *Wasps*, 220   μινυρίζοντες μέλη
                ἀρχαιομελισιδωνοφρυνιχήρατα.

[2] I suspect, however, that many of the lyrics of Sophocles also
ought really to be regarded as based on an Ionic four-syllable foot
($\cup\cup--$ or $-\cup-\cup$ or $--\cup\cup$), treated with great freedom as in
late Asiatic love-songs: e.g. O.C. 1044 ff., *El.* 823 ff., and especially
O.C. 510–34 and O.C. 176–81 = 192–6. Cf. *Athen.* p.697*c.* and
Powell, Collect. Alexandrina, p. 184. Sophocles had, of course, many
Ionic characteristics.

CHAPTER III

AESCHYLUS AS A POET OF IDEAS: THE MYSTICAL PLAYS, *PROMETHEUS* AND *SUPPLICES*

IT was suggested above that Aeschylus, like Euripides, is a poet of ideas: that is to say, he is one of those who derive their inspiration in a large degree from their philosophical beliefs or speculations. Indeed, it is largely through this passionate interest in the problems of the world or of human life that he is able to achieve what is here called the creation of tragedy. In each of the myths or legends that he treats he sees a conflict, and in each conflict he deepens the issues till it becomes one of the eternal problems of life.

Aristophanes chooses him as the antithesis of Euripides, not because Euripides is a philosopher-poet and Aeschylus a pure poet untouched by philosophy, but because Aeschylus represents a philosophical outlook markedly opposed to that of his successor. The gulf that lies between them, as Wilamowitz has well said, is the rise and fall of the sophistic movement: that great movement of thought which emancipated Athens from the prison-house of primitive convention and tradition and then, according to Plato, left her for the time being without convictions or gods or faith, and yet, as history proved, ready to build up the sublime and undying philosophies of the fourth century. Our valuation for good or evil of the work of the great Sophists will depend on our general attitude of mind towards the world. It is satirically summed up in the classic contest in the *Frogs*: e.g.

EURIPIDES

Next, I taught all the town to talk with freedom.

AESCHYLUS

     I admit it:

'Twere better, ere you taught them, you had died amid their curses.

EURIPIDES

I gave them canons to apply, and squares for marking verses:
Taught them to see, think, understand, to scheme for what they wanted;
To fall in love, think evil, question all things. . . .

AESCHYLUS

Granted, granted!

EURIPIDES

I put things on the stage that came from daily life and business,
Where men could catch me if I tripped, could listen without dizziness
To things they knew and judge my art. . . .

Dionysus as judge admits the truth of this questionable claim. Euripides did teach people to do these things:

  Whereas, before they took his school,
  Each sate at home, a simple, cool,
  Religious, unsuspecting fool,
    And happy in his sheep-like way!

So far one would get the impression of Aeschylus as a quiet religious conservative. But the phrase, if true in a sense, is misleading. If Aeschylus is to be called 'conservative' one must, of course, remember that in a highly intellectual republican democracy a Conservative is a republican, a democrat, and an intellectual. Probably we may take Aeschylus as representing the generation which rejoiced in the expulsion of the Tyrants, exulted in the establishment of the Athenian democracy and the new access to 'wisdom' and enlightenment which came with it, and enabled the 'free men' of Marathon to repel the 'slaves' of the terrible King. He would have the same enthusiasm as Herodotus for ἰσονομίη and ἰσηγορίη, 'equal laws' and 'free speech'. He states in the *Persae* (243) the proud claim of the free law-abiding Greeks which is afterwards expressed at greater length and with a Spartan colour by Herodotus.[1] Xerxes asks the exiled Spartan Demaratus how the Spartans can possibly stand against his vastly superior force: 'If indeed they were ruled by one master in our fashion they might perhaps through terror of him become braver than it was their nature to be; or if they were driven by the lash they might go forward to face superior numbers. But, being left loose and at liberty, they obviously cannot do either.' Demaratus answers: 'Though free, they are not free in all things.

[1] vii. 103-4.

There is a master over them called Law, whom
they fear more than thy people fear thee. They
do whatever he commands; and there is one thing
on which he always insists, that they must not fly
from any multitude of men in battle but stay at
their post and either win the victory or die.'

We have two isolated bits of evidence, if evidence they can be called, as to the attitude of
Aeschylus towards contemporary politics. In the
Eumenides he glorifies the Court of the Areopagus
as a tribunal such as exists in no other land from
Pelops' realm to Scythia, 'august, incorruptible,
quick to strike, a watcher over my people while
they sleep' (*Eum.* 702 ff.). The play was produced
in 458 B.C., soon after Ephialtes and Pericles had
greatly reduced the powers of the Areopagus and
confined its jurisdiction to cases of homicide. It
may therefore be thought that Aeschylus writes
as an aristocrat glorifying the great institution
which the democratic party had harshly attacked.
On the other hand, he expressly shows how the
Areopagus was founded to deal with a case of
homicide, shows it so dealing, and makes no suggestion that it ought to have wider powers. So it
may be that he is supporting Pericles, by showing
how great an institution the Court of Areopagus
is, even when confined to the limits of its original
function. Considering that the strong tradition in
the higher kind of Greek poetry, as in good poetry
almost everywhere, was to avoid all the disturbing

irrelevances of contemporary life, I see no evidence of any political allusion in the *Eumenides*. At most one may suspect that the deep longing for peace and concord expressed in the lyrics towards the end of the play and in some of Athena's speeches may be the result of emotions stirred by the conflicts of the time.[1] That is a very different thing from political allusion.

The other passage amounts to nothing more than a guess by Aristophanes at the line Aeschylus would have been likely to take, or could be effectively represented as taking, in contrast to Euripides, had they both been alive in the year 406 B.C. When the two poets are asked what should be done about Alcibiades, Euripides answers:

> I curse that burgher who to help his state
> Is slow, but swift to do her deadly hate,
> With much wit for himself but none for her. . . .

Aeschylus on the contrary says:

> No lion's whelp within thy precincts raise,
> But if it *be* there, bend thee to its ways.

That is, Euripides is against the unprincipled politician; Aeschylus is for supporting the troublesome man of genius. The two views are opposed, and are possibly characteristic of the two poets; but it must be remembered that they are only guesses at what the poets might have said, and that Aeschylus was dead before Alcibiades was heard of.

[1] 976 ff., 858 ff.

The two are next asked in general terms what steps they advise in order to save the country. Euripides answers:

Where Mistrust now has sway put Trust to dwell,
And where Trust is, Mistrust; and all is well.

Presently he explains more clearly that the extreme democrats now entrusted with power should be turned out and a more enlightened moderate government put in. Aeschylus asks a question or two. 'Whom does the City choose for her servants? The Good?' No, she hates them. 'And likes the Bad?' No, but has to put up with them. 'Then there is no help at all that way. The only hope is to fight like the Devil.'

Her one hope is to count her enemy's land
Her own; aye, and her own her enemy's;
Her ships her treasure and her treasure dross.

There is no difference in party politics here. We may be fairly sure that Aeschylus would have disliked the Cleon-Hyperbolus-Cleophon democrats as much as Euripides and Aristophanes himself and almost all the rest of our authorities; but there is something clever and persuasive in the suggestion that while Euripides would be wrapped up in the moral and intellectual problems of government and eager to have men in power who were more ἀγαθοί, or χαρίεντες, or even Δίκαιοι, the old 'Marathon-fighter' would have been more inclined to lose his patience with all the politicians and say: 'No one can prevent these rascals struggling for place and power; but we can at least go and fight the Spartans.'

If Aristophanes makes Aeschylus concentrate upon the war, that certainly does not mean that he regards him as a patron of the War Party. Had he been that, Aristophanes would never have had a good word for him. It only means that he had fought at Marathon, and the 'Men of Marathon' were accepted as the type of tough old fighters whom nothing could daunt. Similarly, his *Seven against Thebes* was described by Gorgias as a drama 'brimming with Ares'[1], and his epitaph, written by himself, while not mentioning his poetry at all, says that as for his soldierly quality 'that can be told by the Grove of Marathon and the long-haired Mede who knows'. He was doubtless a good soldier.

Yet, like many other good soldiers, he certainly hated war and preached peace almost as passionately as Euripides. Athena indeed, being a war-goddess, has to tell the Athenians that, if only they will not fight one another, she can promise them plenty of glorious fights abroad.[2] But the *Seven* gives an amazing picture of what War means to women, its cruelty, its insanity, its blasphemy against God.[3] And in the *Supplices* not only does the King speak of War, in whatever form, as an

---

[1] Quoted in Frogs 1021: Δρᾶμα ποιήσας Ἄρεως μεστόν. Ποῖον; τοὺς ἔπτ᾽ ἐπὶ Θήβας. Cf. Plutarch, *Quaest. Symp.*, p. 715E.

[2] *Eum.* 864–6.   [3] See especially 321–68.

evil to be avoided at almost any cost, but the
Danaids amid their blessings upon Argos, surprise
one a little by praying that she may both observe
her own constitution and grant arbitration treaties
to foreign Powers.[1]

In the matter of teaching and general outlook,
I think the real antithesis to Aeschylus was not
Euripides, but the intellectuals and Sophists of a
rather later age, the kind of young Sophists against
whom Plato and, indeed, Euripides himself protest
so passionately. One sees them at their liveliest in
Plato's *Gorgias*. The development is one which has
often been repeated in ages of great intellectual
activity. Vigorous minds begin to question the
convention in which they have been brought up
and which they have now outgrown. They reject
first the elements in them that are morally repul-
sive, then the parts that are obviously incredible;
they try to reject the husk and preserve the kernel,
and for a time reach a far higher moral and intellectual standard than the generations before them
or the duller people of their own time. Then, it
seems, something is apt to go wrong. Perhaps a
cynic would say—and it would be hard to confute
him—the element of reason in man is so feeble
a thing that he cannot stand successfully except
when propped in the stiff harness of convention.

[1] 437–54; 701 ff.
> To strangers and strange lands let them afford
> Without long strife, Law and the healing word;
> And Justice grant ere any draw the sword.

At any rate, there is always apt to come a later generation which has carried doubt and scepticism much farther and finds the kernel to consist only of inner layers of husk and then more husk, as the place of George IV's heart, according to Thackeray, was supplied by waistcoats and then more waistcoats. First comes inspiration and the exultation of breaking false barriers: at the end comes the mere flabbiness of having no barriers left to break and no talent except for breaking them. It is like the passage from Tolstoy to Artsibashev: from Goethe to Wedekind: from John Stuart Mill to—well, one of several contemporary names may be left to suggest itself. Aeschylus was extremely interested in the ultimate problems of the world. He saw the utter insufficiency and unworthiness of a great deal of the traditional Greek religion, but he took the rest with immense seriousness. Euripides, like many of his generation, had advanced much farther than that; the young lions of Plato's time had reached the final limit.

One is almost ashamed to speak about the religious ideas of Aeschylus, so much has already been written on the subject, and so little of the criticism stands the test of time. Still, they cannot well be left out. It is noteworthy in the first place that there is very little of the regular Homeric Olympianism in Aeschylus, and almost none of the conventional Olympian mythology. Homer, of course, used it freely. Sophocles in the *Electra*

lets his heroine defend her father's memory by
means of a merely mythological story about his
having shot a doe sacred to Artemis. Euripides
in the *Trojan Women* (914 ff.) makes Helen talk
mythology; but that is because she is lying, which
makes all the difference. Aeschylus hardly uses
that kind of material at all. It could not be used
quite seriously, and he was always serious. It is
hard to sum up these things in a generalization;
but one might say that, on the one hand, he does
accept the moral reformation implied in Olympianism, that is; the substitution of human and
humane beings, who can love man and understand
his best thoughts, for the blind and monstrous
forces of the pre-Hellenic, or as Herodotus calls it,
the 'Pelasgian' religion; while, on the other hand,
he makes almost no use of the elaborate mythology
about the Olympians which Homer and many
poets down to the Alexandrians have treated as
such a rich quarry for poetical diversion and
ornament.

The real working religion of Greece and of the
whole Mediterranean world throughout antiquity
was based, as Sir James Frazer has abundantly
shown, on the seasons and the food supply, and
this is especially true of Tragedy, which related
the 'sufferings' or 'experiences' (πάθη) of Dionysus
or some other form of the Vegetation-spirit. It
leads the fifth-century writers to see life in what
I have called elsewhere 'the tragic pattern'—life

leading to death, pride to downfall, or sin to retribution. The sequence is sometimes a moral sequence of transgression and punishment, sometimes it is a mere physical sequence which, if explained at all in theological terms, can be roughly attributed to the supposed jealousy of God.

Aeschylus is constantly occupied with the problem, and in one important passage of the *Agamemnon* insists explicitly on denying this supposed jealousy of God and on moralizing the whole process.[1]

> A grey word liveth, from the morn
>   Of old time among mortals spoken,
> That man's Wealth waxen full shall fall
> Not childless, but get sons withal;
> And ever of great bliss is born
>   A tear unstaunched and a heart broken.

But I hold my thought alone and by others unbeguiled;
'Tis the deed that is unholy shall have issue, child on
    child,
Sin on sin, like his begetters; and they shall be as they
    were.
But the man who walketh straight, and the house
    thereof, tho' Fate
        Exalt him, the children shall be fair.

But Old Sin loves, when comes the hour again,
        To bring forth New,
Which laugheth lusty amid the tears of men;
Yea, and Unruth, his comrade, wherewith none
May plead nor strive, which dareth on and on,

---

[1] *Ag.* 750 ff. The same view is expressed in some of the Hebrew prophets: e.g. Ezekiel xviii; Jeremiah xxxi. 29–30.

Knowing not fear nor any holy thing:
Two fires of darkness in a house, born true,
    Like to their ancient spring.

But Justice shineth in a house low-wrought
    With smoke-stained wall,
And honoureth him who filleth his own lot;
But the unclean hand upon the golden stair
With eyes averse she flieth, seeking where
    Things innocent are; and, heeding not the power
Of wealth by man misgloried, guideth all
    To her own destined hour.

It would be easy to quote many more passages in illustration of this eternal preoccupation of Greek tragedy, and especially the tragedy of Aeschylus, with the thought of Judgement, Δίκη. It is always connected with Μοῖρα, that due Portion which belongs to a man: his share in the tribal land, in the harvest, in the spoils of battle, in honour, and in all the natural joys and sorrows of life. Every man, and indeed every living thing, has a *Moira*; we claim more than our *Moira*, and commit *Hubris*; then *Dikê* casts us back. We try to escape from our *Moira*, but our *Moira* always overtakes us. Other people constantly invade our *Moira* and try to rob us of things: they are committing *Hubris*, and *Dikê* will get them. It is all an affair of Time, Χρόνος, and, so to speak, of Ripeness. Time when it is ripe brings Justice; Time vindicates the *Moira*. And it is no good expecting things before the fullness of Time.

There is, however, one idea, derived directly from the Year-cults, which is raised by Aeschylus to a position of the highest significance. I mean the idea of the 'Third Saviour', or, more correctly, the Saviour who comes Third. One can take the cycle of the years or seasons either in sets of two or sets of three. Taken in sets of two it is continuous: Osiris the wheat-god, Dionysus the vine-god, Attis the pine-tree, Linos the flax, are all in their different ways slain, torn in pieces, crushed, or cut down by their respective enemies. They are wept over with public lamentations. Then they can be reborn or rediscovered in the next year, greeted with joy, and again cut down. The enemy is commonly perhaps winter, or the parching sun, according to climate, but may merely be the reaper with the sickle. There is no place in this sequence for a 'Third Saviour'. Taken in sets of three, however, we have first the existing Year-god or King, the life of the world blooming. Then comes the enemy—the cold, the drought, or the reaper, who slays him, and leaves the world dead and mankind without hope. He is second. Then in the new spring comes the third of the series, the new life of the flocks and fields, the Saviour, who rescues the world from death.

The most remarkable use of this conception by Aeschylus is in the *Oresteia*, where he interprets it by the character of Zeus: Zeus had the regular epithet of 'Saviour' and 'Third Saviour', and was

given, before a function, the third or crowning
libation. Aeschylus states in so many words that
Zeus is the Third King of the Universe. First
came one unnamed—presumably Ouranos—who
was all battle and brute strength: then a second,
his enemy, who otherthrew him and cast him out
to oblivion; then he too met his 'third-thrower',
τριακτήρ—a metaphor from the three bouts of a
wrestling match—and has passed away. The 'third-
thrower' is Zeus, and he is not like the others.
Where they could only smite and be smitten, Zeus
could think. He could therefore learn by suffering,
or by experience, and thus he can save the world.

This conception of the Saviour was a dangerous
leaven fermenting in the orthodoxy of ancient
thought. As long as the Saviour is merely agri-
cultural or seasonal there is no moral difficulty.
There is only anxiety when the old god is dead,
lest the new god should by some mistake fail to be
born, and all the crops perish. There is no condemnation of the moral government of the world.
But in the later developments of Greek thought,
as is well known, Saviour religions developed with
immense vigour, and the reason of their success
was just that, without some Saviour, the government of the world seemed evil and the lot of mankind intolerable. Hence the widespread worship
of Asclepios, the divine Healer; of Mithras the
Redeemer, of Serapis the Saviour, of the many
'Deliverers' of Hermetism and Gnosticism. It is

significant that Zeus Sotêr, so prominent in the
fifth century, tends at this later time to be forgotten. How could Zeus be the Saviour? From
whom did Man want a Saviour if not from the
terrible Ruler of the World himself? It will be
remembered, perhaps, that in some of the most
important forms of Gnosticism, as combined with
Christianity, Jesus was the Saviour of mankind
from the unjust rule of God the Father, who was
identified with the Evil One. That is why Jesus
was made to suffer. In other forms the *Archontes*
or Rulers, who inhabit or inform the Seven Planets
are the oppressors of mankind; the Redeemer,
whoever he is, will eventually escape them and
rise above them.

Like most religious ideas, these conceptions are
probably far older than their first explicit appearance in literature. The main religious ideas of
man are very few in number, mostly continuous
from very early times and almost never original.
It used to be said with confidence, for example,
that astrology made its first appearance in Greece
when Berossus, the Babylonian, set up his school
in Cos about the year 270 B.C.; yet both Aeschylus
and Euripides speak of 'the shaft of a star' and
Aeschylus speaks of the planets as 'bright poten-
tates or rulers'.[1] Evidently a belief in the influence
of the stars was current long before Berossus. It
is much the same with the Saviour religions.

---

[1] ἀστρῶν βέλος *Hip.* 530, *Ag.* 365; λαμπροὺς Δυνάστας *Ag.* 6.

We have noticed that in accepting as a fact the Tragic Pattern, in which all life waxes and then wanes and dies, Aeschylus in the *Agamemnon* passionately claims it as a moral order. He refuses to believe that great bliss or wealth, in itself, leads to a fall; wealth can be innocent, and then provokes no Nemesis. It is wealth combined with injustice or unholiness that alone leads to destruction. The very emotion with which he utters this statement is a sign that Aeschylus is troubled in mind. It shows how intensely he would like to believe that the ways of Fortune are strictly in accordance with morality; that in real life one never does see the righteous forsaken nor his seed begging their bread. He would hardly feel the need to state his belief so strongly if he did not feel the difficulty of believing it, so there is really no deep-seated contradiction when in the *Prometheus* Aeschylus sternly arraigns the world and its unjust Ruler.

It is indisputable that, in regions where the conscience or the social instincts of man are not in control, the ordinary working of the world is nonmoral. It is, as far as one can see, totally indifferent to justice. Our ancestors tried to believe in ordeals which would distinguish the innocent from the guilty; but experience seems to show that the sun shines equally on the righteous and the unrighteous: fire burns them, water drowns them, arsenic poisons them both with absolute

impartiality. Nay, if one begins to criticize by
human standards the moral order implied in a
world where no creature lives except by daily in-
flicting pain and death on others, it is quite easy to
come to the conclusion that the world is definitely
evil. Most religions indeed condemn this temporal
world, but swamp its badness in the alleged infinite goodness of some other: only very few
arraign the Ruler of the World for his present
tyranny. This, however, is the theme of the
Prometheus. We are shown the pitiful state of
mankind. Zeus had hidden away the means of
life[1] from man, just as he had hidden away fire.
He had let loose innumerable winged evils; the
air and sea are full of them; there is no escaping
them. Life is hard and lies always under the
shadow of death. And, after all, for reasons good
or bad, Zeus has from time to time entertained the
idea of destroying man altogether, as a noxious
and unhappy beast. That is what he sought when
he brought about the Trojan War. That is what he
was going to do when Prometheus thwarted him.

So Aeschylus reaches the conception of a
supreme Tyrant, the enemy of man, ruling the
world, and of a champion of mankind, standing
up against him. We have already noticed the
scene of his crucifixion upon the rock. The champion is utterly inferior in strength to Zeus: the
gods too are with Zeus, except the Old Dynasty

---

[1] κρύψαντες γὰρ ἔχουσι θεοὶ βίον ἀνθρώποισιν Hes. *Op.* 42.

that has long since been cast out to desolation.
The only ally of Prometheus is Man himself, Man
the creature of a day, utterly strengthless, dream-
like, who can bring no help except his affection
and συμπαθεία. The true sources of strength that
Prometheus has are his immortality and his in-
domitable will. Zeus can bind him and torture
him; he cannot make him die and cannot break
his resolution.

Συμπαθεία is a stronger word than our 'sympathy', just as its Latin equivalent *compassio* is
stronger than our 'compassion'. It means 'fellow-
suffering' or 'suffering together'. One of the
most sublime of the Stoic doctrines was the συμπαθεία τῶν ὅλων, the conception that every joy or
pain felt by an individual soul vibrates through the
universe, so that with any great martyr or Saviour
the whole of life suffers. This idea finds perhaps
its earliest expression in one of the songs of the
Daughters of Ocean in the *Prometheus*: they suffer
with him, the whole world suffers, and the fiercest
and wildest of men are heart-sore because of him.

CHORUS

A great cry hath risen from the whole world's compassion;
   The peoples of the sunset, they go grieving by the sea
For a beauty long ago, for a greatness of old fashion,
   Thine and thy brethren's, in the days when ye were
     free.
In the Lords of Holy Asia there is wakened a strange
     passion,
    And the lips of them that perish pine for thee.

Yea, the Amazons, the dwellers beyond Phasis,
　Who love not, who battle without fear;
And the hordes that wander in fierce places
　At the world's rim, the Scythians of the Mere;
And hard men, of Araby the flower,
　Where the high crags of Caucasus advance,
They groan in their mountain-builded tower,
　Amid great wrath and flashing of the lance.

． 　 ． 　 ． 　 ． 　 ． 　 ．

The breakers of the sea clash and roar
Together; and the gulfs thereof are sore
With longing. There is murmur of hearts aching
　In Hades and the Cavern of the Deep;
And the torrents of the hills, white-breaking,
　For pity of thy pain weep and weep.

The Daughters of Ocean weep for him; they
love him; but why, why was he so mad as to
champion such a weak, transitory thing as mankind and expect it to be his ally against the
omnipotent? For their own part, they have always
lived in piety and obedience to Zeus in their quiet
home by the Ocean stream (526 ff.):

It were happiness to live thus for ever,
　Untroubled, without fear of things to be,
Making joy by the music of the river;
　But I tremble as mine eyes turn to thee,
　　And I know the long chain
　　Of thy torments, pain on pain;
Thou hast feared not, thou hast trusted to the thought
　　of thine own brain,
　And loved Man so dearly!—What is he?
Alas, the vain service unrepaid,
O Friend! Whither lookest thou for aid?

Shall they comfort thee who perish in a day?
Didst thou see not, that man was ever thus,
Little-doing, and his strength hazardous
    And dream-like? In such weakness, every way,
His blind tribes are chainèd, and his thought
    Shall escape not the prison, nor outstray
The frame the great Carpenter hath wrought.

We have seen before the enmity of Zeus against mankind, and the crucifixion of the Friend of man. We have here the *sympatheia* or fellow-suffering of all creation with Prometheus, and the utter helplessness of man and his champion against the tyrant God. That, then, is the situation in the *Prometheus Desmôtês*: that is the conflict. It seems at first sight insoluble, and before considering the solution that Aeschylus has actually proposed, it may be as well to look for a moment at some of the other solutions that have been propounded in the great literatures of the world.

I think there can be no doubt that the moral sense of civilized man, or of anything that claims the flattering title of *Homo sapiens* in whatever stage of development, is at times shocked and bewildered by the behaviour of the external world. He is its slave, and it cares nothing for him: its values are not his values; and the more he thinks of the world as alive and acting by conscious quasi-human will, the more profoundly is he shocked. The fires, floods, and famines, the great inevitable miseries of nature, are not things which any good man would think of causing or permitting even against his worst enemies, if he had control over them. The rebellion of certain religions against the Ruler of the World, so far as the ordinary run of events can serve as evidence of his character and intentions, is a rebellion of the moral sense not exactly against facts, but against the claim that facts because they are facts must be good. It is to a large extent the protest of the 'rebel passion', Pity, and has led to much fine imaginative work. In itself, the rebellion is not a solution of any difficulty; but it often leads to interesting attempts at solving the main problem.

One of the most impressive, no doubt, is the *Book of Job*. The course of thought in *Job*, though often sublime, is not on the whole lucid, a fact which has led critics to conclude that it is a good deal interpolated. But the main lines can be made out. It is a 'theodicy', an attempt to 'justify the ways of God to man'. Its dramatic form, as well as its philosophical substance, is without parallel in our remains of Hebrew literature. And we may remember that some Biblical scholars have thought it was actually inspired by the *Prometheus* of Aeschylus, which the author may have read, or heard about, in Egypt. The book begins with a mythological setting in which the story is represented as the result of a sort of bet upon the part of Satan that, though Job while prosperous is perfectly pious, he can be made to 'curse God' if

he is sufficiently tormented and afflicted. The
Almighty enters into the spirit of this atrocious
proposal, and every kind of torment is showered
upon the innocent man. It is like torturing your
faithful dog to see if you can make him bite you.
So much for the mythological prologue. Then
comes the real substance of the book. It is a discussion of the just or unjust government of the
world. Through most of the book the divine
Justice is taken for granted, which seems to imply
the conclusion that, since Job is made miserable
by Jehovah, he must be wicked. He must deserve
all that he gets. This is the view of the Comforters,
but Job never admits it. Like the faithful dog,
who will never turn against his master, he says
'Though He slay me, yet will I trust in Him',[1] but
he steadfastly refuses to confess to sins that he has
not committed or to a general wickedness of which
he is not conscious. He cannot see the justice or
the reason of his afflictions; he states his innocence
and craves a reply. He would like to see the case
against him in black and white (xxxi, 35): 'Oh
that one would hear me! Behold, my desire is
that the Almighty should answer me and that
mine adversary had written a book.'

Elihu the Buzite is thoroughly shocked by this
attitude of Job. His belly becomes like wine that
has no vent; it is ready to burst with indignation,
like new bottles. He undertakes to make an

---

[1] So the AV: the original is obscure.

answer. God must be righteous and cannot do
wrong. Therefore Job is committing a grave sin
in protesting his innocence, and thus attempting
to judge the justice of God. 'Thinkest thou this
to be right, that thou saidst My righteousness is
more than God's?' He goes on to argue that God
owes Job nothing: Job's goodness cannot benefit
Him nor Job's wickedness hurt Him. It is exactly
the view rejected by Plutarch[1] but reasserted by
certain medieval theologians, that animals have no
cause to complain if man tortures them, because
he has no duties towards them. On moral grounds
this is a pretty miserable answer, yet it is essentially the same as the answer made by Jehovah
Himself. 'Who is this that darkeneth knowledge?
. . . . Where wast thou when I laid the foundations
of the earth? Declare, if thou hast understanding.
Who hath laid the measures thereof? . . . . Where-
upon are the foundations fashioned? Or who laid
the corner stone thereof when the morning stars
sang together and all the sons of God shouted for
joy?' Later on, after long insistence on the puny
and ephemeral nature of Job, the Almighty comes
to the central argument: 'Wilt thou disannul My
judgment? Wilt thou condemn Me that thou
mayest be righteous? Hast thou an arm like God
or canst thou thunder with a voice like Him?'

   If Plato or Aristotle had been present at this
discussion I think they would have felt as explo-

---

[1] *De Sollertia Animalium,* and more seriously, *De Esu Carnium.*

sive as Elihu the Buzite, but on different grounds.
They would have pointed out that Jehovah was
not answering the real question at all. No one had
doubted God's power, it was His justice they had
questioned; and His only answer has been to
reassert His power again and again in a storm of
magnificent rhetoric, and demand how a worm
like Job dares to ask any question at all. God does
not show, or even say, that He is righteous by
human standards of righteousness; what he does
assert is that He is, in Nietzsche's phrase,
Jenseits von Gut und Böse, and that the puny
standards by which man judges right and wrong
simply do not apply to the power that rules
the universe. If God's rule conflicts with human
morality, that is because human morality is such
a limited thing, not valid beyond particular
regions of time and space. It is impertinence in
man to expect God to be 'righteous'. This can be
defended as a real and profound answer. But it is
one that would have utterly shocked Plato or
Aristotle. The democratic Greek instinctively
cared more for Law and Justice, Νόμος and
Δικαιοσύνη. The Oriental, accustomed to the
rule of a despot or patriarch, cared most for
obedience to the supreme Power.

Let us consider next the line taken by the more
rebel thinkers, some of them proposing solutions,
and some merely denouncing the government of
the world without condescending to propose any

solution at all. Some of the Gnostics considered the present government of the world evil, but believed that some Saviour, some Simon or Jesus or Divine Man, would eventually rescue the Lost Soul of Man, or the Virgin of Divine Wisdom, now wandering lost in the waste of matter, and rise with her to a sphere above the planets. He would in the end conquer the present tyrants of the world, and the rule of Righteousness, or at least the rule of the Saints, be established. Similarly, certain persecuted medieval sects derived from the Hussites in central Europe concluded that since the Pope persecuted them and was the representative of God upon earth, therefore God also was a persecutor and an enemy; the only trustworthy champion of the oppressed was God's conquered and injured rival, Satan; though perhaps there was also something to be hoped from Jesus, whom God had had crucified because he was kind to man. There are echoes of these ideas in various imaginative writers of the 'demoniac' school, from Byron and Leopardi to Anatole France. There was a very striking play called *Prometheus* begun by Goethe in his youth. It was unfortunately shown at an early stage to Lessing and other critics, who were shocked and urged the author to suppress it. Consequently, it is still a fragment and little known.

To English readers, of course, the most famous poem on this subject is Shelley's *Prometheus Un-*

bound. It is strongly influenced by Aeschylus, and, in a less degree, by Milton. Shelley, however, has moralized the whole issue far more than either of his models. Aeschylus had taken a folk-tale about the contest between a cunning minor god and a powerful high god, and turned it into the contest between a Friend of Man and the Supreme Ruler who despises man. Shelley starts from this stage, and makes his Friend of Man a personification of Love and the Christian virtues, while the Supreme Ruler becomes a power of Supreme Evil. It is surprising that out of material so undramatic as a mere contest between pure evil and pure good Shelley has made such a magnificent poem. It leaves him, however, with an even more steep and pronounced problem to solve: a problem which cannot be solved either on Job's lines or—as we shall see—on those of Aeschylus. There is nothing for Shelley to do except boldly to make Zeus fall and Prometheus reign—or at least initiate a sort of anarchist republic of triumphant virtue in which there is no need of a ruler. The plain man's objection to this as a solution is that it is obviously not true. The non-human government of the world is not overthrown, and shows no signs of being likely to be overthrown. Also, the plain man might say, even if the way of the world is not quite agreeable to the demands of the human conscience, it is not as purely black as Shelley makes out. On the other hand, we must remember that

Shelley definitely believed in the perfectibility of man as a practical proposition. He believed that its consummation was quite feasible, and only prevented from coming to immediate realization by certain 'customs' and 'prejudices' which could be corrected or removed by 'enlightenment'. He did probably think that a state more or less resembling that universal bliss described in the last Act of *Prometheus* would actually be some day achieved by mankind. One might possibly make the Shelleian conception credible in the following way. Take the existing world as a cockpit of strife and cruelty, in which every living thing lives daily by the death and torment of another and innocence is of no value: that is Zeus. In the midst of that hell, however, there exists the plain undeniable fact of love and self-sacrifice, as shown, for example, in the devotion of a tigress to her cubs and the φιλία, friendship or social instinct, which binds society together: that is Prometheus. It is a very weak, very small, ingredient in the whole mass, but it looks as if it was increasing. In course of time, say, in a hundred million years or so, the time which light from the farthest star takes to reach the earth, it may have grown so strong as to prevail completely. That would be Shelley's Promethean reign, reached by endurance and effort.[1]

[1] To endure pangs which hope thinks infinite;
To forgive wrongs darker than death or night;

But what was the solution propounded by Aeschylus himself? We know that it was not the fall of Zeus. The threats of Prometheus are strong, but, as we have already seen, they are all conditional. Zeus must fall unless Prometheus reveals the secret that will save him, and this Prometheus will not reveal except on his own conditions. No threat of torture will move him. His present punishment is not enough, and he is hurled in chains to Tartarus. That is the state of affairs at the end of the *Prometheus Bound*, which was the first play of a tragic trilogy.

The second was called Προμηθεὺς Λυόμενος, not *Prometheus Unbound*, but *The Unbinding of Prometheus*, since λυόμενος is a present participle. The play itself is lost, but there are some twenty references to it in ancient literature, and we can make out something of its plot. There was a Chorus of Titans sympathizing with Prometheus, like the Daughters of Ocean in the *Prometheus Bound*. Among the characters were Gaia, the mother of Prometheus, and Heracles. Now, it was Gaia who revealed to Prometheus the secret on which the fate of Zeus depended. It therefore seems highly

> To defy power that seems omnipotent;
> To love and bear, to hope till hope creates
> From its own wreck the thing it contemplates;
> Never to change nor falter nor repent;
> This, like thy glory, Titan, is to be
> Good, great and joyous, beautiful and free;
> This is alone life, power, empire and victory.
> Shelley, *Prometheus*, last lines.

probable that she has come in order to be author-
ized by Prometheus to reveal it to Zeus. It was
Heracles who set Prometheus free; he must be
there by the will of Zeus in order to do so. The
secret is that the son of Thetis will be greater than
his father. Zeus had been on the point of making
her his bride, but on hearing this oracle he hands
her over to a mortal suitor, Pêleus. Thus Zeus
is saved: he is not to have a son greater than himself. In return he sets Prometheus free, restores
his dignities, and founds in his honour the Festival
of the Promethia. This festival seems to have been
the subject of the third play, the Προμηθεὺς Πυρφόρος, *Prometheus the Fire-bearer*.[1] That, then, is
the end of the story. Peace is made on certain
terms between the two enemies, and solemnized
in a great ritual, as in the *Eumenides*.

Now, here there is a chance of making a bad
mistake. In the Hesiodic folk-tale, where the
whole story was a contest of wit against power,
with no moral issue at stake, the secret was probably merely a trump card. Zeus, whatever his

---

[1] It has often been thought that πυρφόρος must have meant 'Fire-
bringer' and applied to the first play of the three, describing Prometheus' offence, the bringing of the fire to man. The Scholia, however,
tell us definitely that Aeschylus in the Πυρφόρος says that Prometheus
had been bound for thirty thousand years; it must therefore have been
the closing play of the trilogy, not the opening. The foundation of a
festival was a common ending for tragedies. In Euripides, who wrote
in single plays, it often comes at the end of a single play; in Aeschylus,
who wrote in trilogies, it seems to have been kept as a rule for the last
play of a trilogy.

feelings, was compelled to make terms, and Prometheus insisted on pretty stiff ones—his own release and reinstatement, the same for all the Titans, and some sort of survival rights for mankind. And some scholars have attributed this same dénouement, without qualification, to Aeschylus. I think it is clear that they are wrong. Such a mechanical solution is out of tone with Aeschylus' whole treatment, just as it is in tone with that of Hesiod. Even if we had no external evidence I confess that I should feel such an end to the *Prometheus* trilogy to be incredible. The real solution takes us into one of the deepest and most characteristic recesses of the mind of Aeschylus. It is Zeus who repents more than Prometheus.

The evidence for this statement is to be found in other plays, not in the fragments of the *Prometheus*. We shall find in the *Agamemnon* that, as contrasted with all the previous rulers of Heaven, Zeus has a new and extraordinary faculty: the power to think and to learn by suffering. Before Zeus the world was governed by beings who were like blind forces of nature. But with Zeus came something new: what the Greeks called ξύνεσις or Understanding. He understood. Euripides in the *Frogs* prays to *Sunesis*, 'Understanding'; the Chorus of Huntsmen in the *Hippolytus*, in the midst of their despair, cling to a belief in Ξύνεσίν τινα, 'some great Understanding'; the Old Men in the *Heracles*, more rebellious, ponder how different the world would be if the gods had ξύνεσις like men.[1]

Through this power of thought or understanding Zeus changes his way of rule.[2]

> Zeus, Zeus, Whate'er He be—
>   If this name He love to hear,
> This He shall be called of me.
>   Searching earth and sea and air,
> Refuge nowhere can I find
> Save Him only, if my mind
> Would cast off, before it die,
> The burden of this vanity.
>
> One there was who reigned of old
>   Big with wrath to brave and blast:
> Lo, his name is no more told!
>   And who followed met at last
> The Third Thrower and is gone.
> Only they whose hearts have known
> Zeus, the Conqueror and the Friend,
> They shall win their vision's end:
>
> Zeus the Guide, who made man turn
>   Thoughtward, Zeus who did ordain
> Man by suffering shall learn.
>   So the heart of him, again
> Aching with remembered pain,
> Bleeds and sleepeth not, until
> Wisdom comes against his will.
> 'Tis the gift of One by strife
> Lifted to the throne of life.

What Zeus taught to man he had first practised himself. He came by strife and battle to his throne.

---

[1] *Frogs*, 893; *Hip.* 1105; *Her.* 655.   [2] *Ag.* 160 ff.

He overpowered and imprisoned his adversaries; and then '*aching with remembered pain*', he learned something: something which led him to set free his enemies the Titans, to pardon sinners like Ixion and Orestes, to send Heracles to release Prometheus, and to bring Io at last to peace. Zeus himself is the Saviour.

The key to the understanding of Zeus lies in his healing of Io and his pardon of Orestes. The pardon of Orestes we must deal with later:[1] Io we can consider now.

In the *Prometheus Desmôtês* his treatment of Io is like the last infamy of a licentious tyrant. For the traditional tyrant in Greek poetry behaves like the traditional wicked baronet of the English stage. We have already heard Io's story; and lest there should be any doubt as to the impression made by this conduct of Zeus, we must note that the Chorus are almost inarticulate with horror at such πήματα, λύματα, Δείματα, 'sufferings, crimes, and terrors', while Io herself, on hearing her future fate, breaks into inarticulate sobbing, and then threatens to throw herself over the precipice and die. Prometheus bids her think of him. Her torment is comparatively short: he must suffer on, age after age, until Zeus is hurled from his throne. 'What!' cries Io, 'Can that ever be?' It would be the one thing that could reconcile her to life. Prometheus assures her that it must come;

[1] See Chapter VI.

none but Prometheus himself can speak the word
by which Zeus might be saved, and it is taken for
granted by both Io and Prometheus himself that
that word will never be spoken.

Thus we have in this play Zeus appearing as an
unredeemed tyrant, hating men, torturing their
divine champion, and making women the victims
of his lust. Yet the audience might suspect that
this was not the whole truth, for several reasons.
Not only would they hesitate to expect a thorough-
going Satanism from Aeschylus; they knew that
in the tradition Zeus and Prometheus were, as a
matter of fact, reconciled; and they also knew that
in an earlier play Aeschylus had already treated
the Io story, deepened all its issues, and made of
it a mystery tending to the glory of Zeus in spite
of all.

In the *Suppliant Women*, many years before the
Prometheus, the descendants of Io in the fifth
generation come back from Egypt, where they
were born, to Argos. They claim and receive
protection from the Argives as descendants of an
Argive princess. Why have they come? Because
they are flying across the seas from the lust of
Aegyptus' Sons; and the whole play rings with
denunciations of the unpardonable sin of the pur-
suers.

> Shall bird be clean, which maketh bird his food?
> Shall man be clean, who doth his lust fulfil
> Against her will, against her father's will,

On woman? Never more shall such an one,
Nay, not in death, escape the deed he has done.
A Zeus is there, not ours, on each bowed head
Who deals the unchanging judgment of the dead.

'Against her will, against her father's will' . . . that
is exactly what Zeus himself did to Io. The
daughters of Io 'wander in the print of ancient
feet', and are actually asking for protection against
violation from Zeus, the violator of Io. How is
this strange situation to be met?

In the first place, without directly contradicting
the legend, Aeschylus seems to deny that there
was any lust, any violation. There was λόγος τις,
'a certain story', 'a tradition', telling of such. But
the actual birth of Io's son Epaphus was a Virgin
Birth, by the laying on of the hand of Zeus. And
neither in the *Supplices* nor in the *Prometheus* is
there any mention of an actual union between
Zeus and the mortal woman.

Next, though the sufferings of Io are not at all
minimized, they are treated as a sort of ordeal
or preparation, leading towards some conclusion
which involves ineffable bliss. One must presume
that the end was not to be reached without them;
and the end means not only bliss to Io but the
birth of a Saviour of the World, who is also the
destined liberator of Prometheus. One cannot but
be reminded of the passion of the suffering God
or Redeemer in various of the mysteries.

But it is not very helpful merely to give, as it

were, the skeleton argument of a poem on which
the author has evidently spent intense thought and
emotion. I will quote such translation as I have
been able to make of the lyric in which Aeschylus
treats the Io myth most fully.

> O King of Kings,
> Blest beyond all things blest;
> Of perfect things
> In power the perfectest;
> Hear in thy bliss
> Our prayer, and let it be!
> Keep from us this
> That is abhorred by thee,
> The lust of man; Oh, deep beneath the dark
> Blue water sink that black and evil barque!

> To woman turn thine eye;
> Regard us here:
> The children's child am I
> Of her once dear.
> Remember; understand
> Dear thoughts long dead,
> Thou who didst lay thine hand
> On Io's head!
> From her who once was thine, O Zeus, we come,
> Lost children, seeking Argos and our home.

> I wander in the print of ancient feet;
> 'Mid these same blossoms haunted Io grazed;
> From this same pasture sweet
> She fled, by pain made fleet,
> Through many tribes of men, with mind amazed,
> Till all the fronting world she clove in twain,
> And left deep-scored her pathway o'er the main.

There follows a description of her terrible pilgrimage through many lands, ending in Egypt:

> . . . there must Io go,
>   Mad with long shame and scorn,
> Witness to Hera's greatness, and a cry
> Of torment on her lips like prophecy.
>
>
> Mortals on that day dwelling in the land,
>   Their hearts shook inwardly,
> Seeing a sight they might not understand:
>   In pale fear every eye,
> Gazed on a being agonized, half-human,
> Some part a tortured beast and some part woman:
>   Behold a mystery!
> By whose word at the last was comfort given
> To Io wounded, wandering, gadfly-driven?
>
>
> Thou, Zeus, from everlasting ages Lord,
>   Didst set her free;
> By thine unwounding strength, thy breath in-poured,
>   Wrath ceased to be;
> In a last tenderness of tears her shame
>   Flowed forth to die:
> She took into her body the great Name,
>   The Word that cannot lie,
> And bore a babe most perfect, without blame,
>
>
> Through ages long fulfilled in happiness.
>   Wherefore all Earth
> Lifteth her voice to praise the Father, and bless
>   The supreme birth.
> This is the deed of Zeus, all deeds above,

Who else but He
Could tear the web of hate that Hera wove?
And thus are we, even we,
Born of that wrong, that agony, that love.[1]

This enables us, so far as such intimacy with a
man who has been dead for two thousand years
is possible at all, to grasp the main lines of Aeschylus' thought, and the theory by which he tries
to answer Job's question. First, Zeus has the
power of Thought, the power of Learning by
experience, which differentiates him and his rule
from all that has gone before. He has also led man
along the road of Thought. He learns and does
better. This gives us the interesting theory—not,
like Shelley's, of the perfectibility of Man—but
of the perfectibility of God. The doctrine recurs
in a slightly different form, if I remember rightly,
in the famous pessimist philosopher, Von Hart-
mann, who urges his disciples 'To work with God
to redeem God'. Translated from metaphor into
a statement of fact, Aeschylus' theory would mean
that this brutal non-moral external world which
still dominates Man and shocks his conscience has
itself a possibility of evolving towards something
more spiritual and more concordant with our

---

[1] I will not here discuss the possible meaning of the Io myth as
allegory in the mind of Aeschylus, except to suggest that Io, like all
these cow- or moon-goddesses, typifies the fate of woman: the violation
of virginity, the agony of child-birth, and the love that—so Aeschylus
suggests—atones for all. I have ventured to expand the birth from
Epaphus in the last verse in order to make this point clearer. (See
the Introduction to my translation of the *Suppliant Women*.)

higher ideals—a view which would not, I think,
be rejected by Bergson.

But there is a second element in the theory
also: one which is thrilling as poetry, though in
philosophy it may suggest a mere cowardly volte-
face. What if there is something quite wrong in
the present condemnation of Zeus as he now is?
What if Prometheus and Io herself are utterly
mistaken, at any rate in their judgement of what
seems like his worst action? It is not merely that
at present he is new to the throne, and still—as
we should put it—in a state of war-psychosis, from
which, as he learns, he will recover.[1] Even the
things which he is doing now are part of a long-
distance plan, inscrutable by our mortal minds
and therefore unjudgeable. One can only pray
that his desire may be for what we, so far as we
understand it, should call good or godlike.

To quote the *Supplices* again (86):

Oh, may the desire of God be indeed of God!
  Is it not strong in the chase?
On all roads with dark issue, a burning rod,
  It guides man's mortal race.

It falleth firm, it slippeth not, whatso thought
  In the brain of Zeus is formed. It is word and deed.
Through tangled forest and shadow His paths are
      wrought,
  Which none may trace nor read.

Thus we see that Aeschylus has in his mind two

[1] *Pr.* 35.

speculative answers to the Question of Job, each effective singly but the two still more effective in combination. The world power that he calls Zeus learns and grows. The *élan vital*, as M. Bergson calls it, at first almost blind in its striving, acquires clearer and more definite aims; the striving becomes more intelligent, and at last more spiritual. At the same time, even in its present state, amid all its horrors, the world power is something beyond our comprehension and power of judgement. Though doubtless terribly imperfect even by its own standards, it is not to be fully understood or measured by standards which have been built up to suit the finite and narrow experience of man.

CHAPTER IV

THE WAR PLAYS, *PERSAE* AND
SEVEN AGAINST THEBES

WITH the *Persae* we seem to be on firmer ground than with the *Supplices* or *Prometheus*. For one thing it is not only a play: it is a direct historical record of one of the great events that have decided the destiny of Europe, the repulse of the invasion of Greece by Xerxes. It gives a detailed account of a great sea-battle fought more than two thousand four hundred years ago by one who was not only an eyewitness but a combatant, and one who, besides his Greek sense of poetry, had also the peculiar Greek power of describing what he saw. In some ways his account of the actual Battle of Salamis is better even than that of the historian Herodotus, writing forty years later with an abundance of carefully sifted material. True, the details of the long Persian retreat are much vaguer; Aeschylus knew them only by report. The account of previous Persian history shows how very little was known in 472 even by the best-informed Athenians about the great empire which had almost become their master. Aeschylus knew nothing apparently about Astyages and Cyaxares, he had little of the information at the disposal of Herodotus; but his account of Salamis, the night before, the morning, and the day, and the look

of the shores and shallows on the day after, is that
of an eyewitness of the sort the Greeks called
ἀληθής—'one who does not forget'.

We have also some details about the performance. The Didascalia, or official record of the
performance at Athens, is in part preserved. The
date was the archonship of Menon, 473–472 B.C.;
and since the Great Dionysia took place in the
spring, that clearly takes us to the spring of
472. The *chorêgus*, that is, the citizen responsible
for the expenses, was Pericles. Aeschylus obtained the first prize with the four plays *Phineus*,
Persae, *Glaucus of Potniae*, and *Prometheus the
Firekindler*. We learn further that Aeschylus produced the *Persae* a year or two later at Syracuse,
on the invitation of the Tyrant Hiero.

The list of four plays raises a problem. It was
the custom of Aeschylus to produce a proper
trilogy of continuous plays on the same subject,
followed by a satyr-play. It was so in the *Prometheus* trilogy, the Theban trilogy, the Danaid
trilogy, and finally in the *Oresteia*. Indeed, Suidas
tells us that it was Sophocles who began the practice of competing with separate plays which did
not form a continuous story. This practice had
its obvious advantages, and one would not be
surprised to find that in some of his later work
Aeschylus had followed the younger playwright's
example. But the *Persae* is a very early play; the
earliest but one that we possess. Consequently

one cannot but suspect that the four plays *Phineus*, *Persae*, *Glaucus of Potniae*, and *Prometheus the Fire-kindler* really form some sort of continuous story.

For this last a quite good connexion suggests itself. For when the Greeks returned to their cities after the Battle of Plataea, they had to purify the sacred places which had been polluted by the Persians, and to do this they put out all the fires in the country and had them relit from the sacred hearth at Delphi.[1] That great ceremonial of fire-kindling would be a good subject for the final play of a tetralogy.

As to the first of the four, *Phineus*, that blind prophet is chiefly known for his meeting with the Argonauts, when he was delivered from the harpies by the two Sons of the North Wind. Now Herodotus treats the Argonaut expedition as an invasion of Asia by Europe, duly repaid in course of time by the invasion of Europe by Asia under the Persians.[2] On this view, the *Phineus* would give us the blind prophet foretelling to the Argonauts the retributory war which their bold adventure must bring about: the *Persae* would show the prophecy fulfilled. The third play, *Glaucus of Potniae*,[3] fits in less well. This Glaucus was a hero of the vegetation type, like Dionysus, Osiris,

---

[1] Plut. *Aristides*, 20; *Numa*, 9.

[2] Hdt. i. 2; cf. Aesch. fr. 260 N.

[3] The word Ποτνιεύς is omitted in the best MS. There was another play by Aeschylus, *Glaucus of the Sea*, Πόντιος, which, however, seems from the scanty evidence to have been a satyr-play, not a tragedy.

Pentheus, Orpheus, who died by a *sparagmos*; like Hippolytus, he suffered it from his own horses. He fed his horses on flesh, as the Thracian Lycurgus did, and they went mad and devoured him at the village of Potniae. One can see no direct connexion with the *Persae*, though it is curious that Potniae was close by the site of the Battle of Plataea and was perhaps actually covered by the preliminary skirmish in which the general of the Persian cavalry, Masistios, was killed by the action of his horse. Struck by an arrow, the animal reared and fell on him, and he was then cut to pieces by the enemy.[1] A horse and a *sparagmos*: it is just possible therefore that the *Persae* did form the second play of a connected trilogy and that we can accept Suidas' statement as true. But the connexion was clearly far less close and continuous than in the other Aeschylean trilogies known to us.

The *Persae* is generally described as the first historical play in European literature, and to some extent the description obviously fits. The Battle of Salamis was fought in 480, Plataea in 479; the Athenians rebuilt their ruined city in 478, and soon afterwards celebrated their victory, or rather their deliverance, in a tragedy, the *Persae* of Phrynichus. In 472, i.e. four or five years later, came the *Persae* of Aeschylus, with the same subject and title and, so we are informed by a very ancient authority,[2] a general similarity of treat-

---

[1] Hdt. ix. 20, 24.   [2] Glaucus of Rhegium, *floruit c.* 400 B.C.

ment. One would like to know if there had been
a regular celebration of the same theme at the
Great Dionysia every year between 478 and 472.
It seems quite likely, though evidently the institution was not permanent. There was certainly
a regular celebration every four years at the
Panathenaea, where the epic of Choirilos on the
Persian War was, for a time, allowed the unique
privilege of being recited along with the works
of Homer. There was an annual celebration of
the Victory of Salamis at the Aianteia, or festival
in honour of Ajax, the Salaminian hero, on Muny-
chion 16, about a month after the Dionysia.[1] It
seems therefore a little misleading to speak of the
Persae as an historical play. It is rather a national
celebration. It is not so much to be compared
with a modern play about, say, Mary, Queen of
Scots, as with a Thanksgiving Service at West-
minster Abbey to commemorate the Armistice of
1918 . . . except that the service would of course
be a service and the *Persae* is, after all, a drama.

The construction is extremely simple. It needs
only a Chorus and two actors, and falls into three
distinct parts. At the opening the Persian Elders,
'The Faithful', are at their Council Chamber
waiting for news, long delayed, of the vast armies
that have gone overseas to subdue Hellas. We

---

[1] We hear in later times of a *Tragoedia Persis* by Cleainetos and
Nicomachos; a dithyramb, *Persae*, by Timotheos; also Πέρσαι Σάτυροι
by Anaxion.

hear of the long array of Persian and Median nobles, of vassal kings from Memphis and Egyptian Thebes; Lydian princes, gay with golden armour and four-horsed and even six-horsed chariots, followed by subject tribes from the mountains; and lastly the golden Babylon with her motley multitude of nations, marshmen and rivermen, terrible archers, and 'all the long-knived multitude' from the hidden valleys of Asia. Their hearts rise as they sing. Who could ever stand against such a flood of armed men? War has been from of old the birthright of the Persian; the thunder of the horsemen and the overthrowing of towers and the trampling of cities in the dust. And now, the dry land being conquered, they have turned conquering to the sea.

We have seen the waves whiten in the fury of the wind,
We have faced the holy places of the deep.

And yet . . . the inscrutable craft of God, is Man ever safe from it? It is strange in this empty land; with no news; only the old men and the women left, and the women often weeping for the men who have gone. They are about to take counsel together when there enters to them the Queen Mother, Atossa—who, as Herodotus tells us, 'held at that time all the power'. She has been disturbed by strange dreams and asks for advice. The Elders advise her to pray to her dead husband, Darius, the old and good King, who had visited her in the dream, and are answering her questions about

Athens and the Greeks, what armies they have,
what resources, how, with no master over them,
they can ever face an angry foe, when there rushes
in a Messenger from Xerxes to announce that all
is lost. Salamis—hated name—is crowded with
Persian dead.

The Messenger is at first wild and inarticulate
with grief; then in answer to Atossa's questions he
becomes coherent. Xerxes himself still lives.

> That word is joy to all my house, a bright
> Gleam as of morning after starless night.

But the others—Artembares, Dadochas the chili-
arch, Tenagon the Bactrian are dead; there was
a little island full of wild pigeons where the bodies
were floating. Name after great name we hear of
them, slain some one way and some another.
Atossa questions further: What were the numbers?
Is Athens still unbroken? 'Yes', says the Messenger; 'while her men live she has an unbroken wall.'
As a matter of fact, the town and acropolis had
been sacked and burnt; all Athens was now
in the ships. At last the Messenger tells his full
story of the battle: how a pretended traitor came
secretly to Xerxes to warn him that the Greeks
intended to fly as soon as night fell. Xerxes was
delighted and made his plans for surrounding
them; all the outlets were guarded, ships sent
round to the other side of Salamis, and all the
Persian fleet kept at work, rowing up and down, so
that no Greek vessel should escape. But nothing

happened. No sign came from the Greeks at their anchorage.

> Not till the wild white horses of the Morn
> Took all the earth with glory; then was borne
> A sound across the sea, a voice, a strong
> Clamour exultant like a leaping song,
> And Echo answering from the island rock
> Cried 'Battle'.

The Persians had been enticed into the narrows, where the sea-craft of the Greeks had more scope to crowd them and drive them on one another till their oars were broken by the brazen rams and ship after ship went over. The few escaped who could.

And even that was not the end. Xerxes had taken possession of a little island, Psyttaleia, between Salamis and the mainland, and landed a body of chosen troops there. When the sea-fight was lost, this island became a trap. The Greeks surrounded it and charged

> till no more
> Breathed any life of man upon that shore.
> And Xerxes groaned, looking upon that deep
> Of misery. For a throne he had, a steep
> And towering crest, hard by the open sea,
> Commanding all the field.

He groaned, rent his robes, sent orders of retreat to the land army, and fled. The retreat was long and painful. Command of the sea being lost, there were no means of feeding adequately such

large numbers; winter storms came prematurely,
and of course the route lay mostly through hostile
country.

Atossa goes to prepare her offerings, and after
a great imaginative lyric by the Chorus, wailing
for the men who are 'torn by the awful sea,
gnawed by the voiceless children of the Undefiled', returns in sad garb and without her train
of attendants, to pour the libations to Darius. We
find that we are now at his grave—which was, as
a matter of fact, at Persepolis, some hundreds of
miles away from Susa. Early tragedy paid little
attention to such minutiae. There follows an impassioned scene of Invocation, full of strange
words and oriental colour, till out of the Tomb
arises the ghost or spirit of the Great King. 'Why
have they called him?' The Elders for very dread
cannot speak. He turns to Atossa, who, with the
same dignity and courage that she shows all
through the play, tells him without shrinking the
whole tale of disaster.

It is news to him and yet not news. For he
recognizes in it the fulfilment of an oracle which
he had hoped would be long postponed, but which
had now been precipitated upon Persia by the
Hubris of Xerxes. And the end is not yet. The
crown of suffering is still to come for

Those godless, those of pride infatuate,
Who made of Greece their prey, nor held it shame
To rob her gods and give her shrines to flame.

Altars lie wrecked and images of God
O'erthrown, disbased, and down in rubbish trod.
For which dire sin, dire suffering now is theirs,
And direr yet shall be. . . .
An oozing crust Plataea's field shall know
Of mire blood-soaked beneath the Dorian lance;
And piles of dead dumb warning shall advance,
Even to our children's children, that the eye
Of mortal man lift not his hopes too high.

Hubris against his fellow man, and sacrilege
against the gods: the two sins for which *Moira*
and *Dikê* inevitably exact atonement. Darius
takes his way again to the darkness, after bidding
Atossa go to meet Xerxes, who is returning in
discomfiture, his rent garments scarcely covering
his body. 'He shall have robes meet for a King!'
cries his mother, and goes.

A strange Chorus of dreams and memory follows, about the greatness and peace of the Persian
Empire in Darius' day; the Greek cities and
islands which are now lost to Persia—or from
another point of view, now free and in alliance
with Athens; the great armies of Persia and the
allies from unnumbered lands, now brought to
nothing, 'scourged by the conquering sea'.

Xerxes enters in lamentation, humiliated yet
still dignified and even generous. He is met by
the Elders with bitter reproaches: Where are
those he took with him, the youth of the land, the
friends who fought at the King's side, where has

he left them, he, the 'Crowder of Hades with Persian dead'? He accepts the full blame.

> I left them dying;
> Fallen I left them,
> From a Tyrian galley
> Fallen and lost.

Yâwân, the despised Ionian, had taken them in his conquering 'shipwallèd battle

> As he swept the dark of the waters
> And the desolate shore'.

The sad procession moves towards the Palace—the scene is before the Palace again, not at Darius' Tomb—through the long streets:

XER. O ye that walked so softly, raise your head,
    Let your grief roam.
CHO. O soil of Persia, thou art hard to tread!
XER. O trireme ships, O shoals of Persian dead!
CHO. With sobs that scarce find voice I lead thee home.

Why is the *Persae* a great tragedy? It has little plot and not much study of character; it was apparently a performance written to order for a public celebration; it was not original—in the ordinary sense at least—but modelled on a previous play of the same title and subject by another author; and lastly, it is a celebration of a national victory, one of the very worst fields for good poetry. How can it be a great tragedy?

To take the last point first, patriotic poetry as a class is not usually good: it is poetry written not to express an essentially poetical impulse or intuition, but poetry used as a vehicle for expressing an alien emotion. It suffers from the same dangers as political or argumentative poetry. The emotion of patriotism may no doubt include highly dramatic and poetical elements; but conquering patriotism hardly ever makes good poetry. One may think of Drayton's *Agincourt*, Dryden's *Annus Mirabilis*, or the long persecution of the Muse which eventually produced Addison's poem on the Battle of Blenheim. The fact is that the emotions of victory—the self-satisfaction of success, the triumphing over opponents, the exultation, the almost inevitable blindness to deeper issues—militate against true poetry. If the victory is felt as an escape or deliverance, the case is different; but otherwise defeat is a deeper experience than victory, as being wounded involves stronger sensations than wounding some one else. Consequently, it is defeat, not victory, that has produced most of the great epics. Shakespeare did well not to write about the defeat of the Armada.

In our time there has been much fine literature generated by the Napoleonic Wars, from Stendhal and Erckmann-Chatrian to Thackeray and Tolstoy. But none are celebrations of mere victory; all are studies of the experiences of the human soul in times of great trial, and this is most markedly true in the greatest of them, *War and Peace*. I am disposed to think that, except possibly the *Song*

of Deborah, a lyrical outburst of primitive emotion, the *Persae* is the only celebration of a victory
in war which reaches the rank of the highest
poetry. Here again, Aeschylus has shown his
power of creating tragedy. As he made the
Prometheus tragedy out of a folk-tale, so here he
makes high poetry out of a public celebration of
victory. If once we can really grasp this quality
in Aeschylus, the quality of deepening and making great all the issues that he touches, we can see
why the *Persae* has overcome—or at least is not
injured by—the other points which might be
expected to tell against it. If it has little plot or
study of character, those are qualities which make
an average play or story interesting and clever;
they are not wanted in the highest imaginative
work and, if present, tend rather to belittle it. In
the mood of high contemplation one does not
want to have the attention diverted to ingenuities.
If it was 'written to order for a public celebration',
so apparently was the *Iliad*. We must accept the
strange fact that an ancient city could be a beloved and beautiful thing, a thing not necessarily
better than a modern municipality, but different
in atmosphere. In the security of modern life we
have outgrown the sanctity of the walled city, as
we have outgrown that of the tribe or family, and
cannot any longer feel about them as the ancients
felt. When man lived surrounded by enemies,
his family were the people who would fight for

him while living and avenge him when dead; his
city was the ringed wall within which he could
breathe in peace and pursue happiness. And as
for the *Persae* being largely modelled on a previous play by another writer, that, one might
almost say, is the normal condition of most great
poetry. The true poet loves the tradition and
rehandles it as his own special love suggests; the
demand that a poet should be original is one of
the eccentricities of modernism. The writer of a
detective story ought to give us 'something new',
but a poet should mostly deal with things that
are not new but eternal.

It is all very well, however, to prove, or at least
to argue, that certain qualities which would certainly be bad in a modern novel need not be so
in the *Persae*. It is more difficult to show in what
ways Aeschylus has in the *Persae* transfigured his
subject and 'created tragedy' out of the story of a
battle not yet ten years old, just as he did out of
folk-tales about the Danaids and Prometheus.

In the first place, we must remember that the
subject of Greek tragedy is always the heroic
saga. It is never an invented story, and it is never
the history of ordinary human beings. I should
doubt if there was any named character in an
Attic tragedy who was not actually in some way
an object of worship: a god or hero or at least the
possessor of some taboo tomb or oracle or ritual.
One of the things that roused such strong criticism

against some of the works of Euripides was not
that he was too 'realistic' in the ordinary sense:
he was certainly not so. It was precisely that he
carried a little farther the natural work of any
dramatist handling traditional religious material.
While keeping the heroic names, he seemed to
make the possessors of those names speak and feel
like normal human beings. Now when Aeschylus,
or Phrynichus before him, put on the stage the
story of a contemporary war, there must have been
a question whether he would bring down tragedy
from its heroic level to that of common life, or
exalt the contemporary story to a legendary greatness. We cannot say what Phrynichus did, but
Aeschylus certainly did the latter. There is a
speech of Themistocles recorded by Herodotus
(viii. 109) after the Battle of Salamis: 'It is not
we who have done these things! It is the gods
and heroes, who grudged that the sovranty of
Asia and Europe should be in the hands of one
proud and impious man.' 'It is not we who have
done these things!' That is the expression of the
emotion of a great moment. The Greeks were
delivered; the deliverance was a thing incredible;
it must be the work of God, not of Man. The
first secret of the *Persae* is that Aeschylus pre-
serves that emotion from beginning to end.

It is the work of the gods, not of man: not of
Aristides, nor Themistocles, nor Pausanias, not
even of the Spartans or Athenians. Consequently

not a single Greek individual is mentioned in the *Persae*. This was clearly right. If one Greek general had been named the play would have become modern and been exposed to all the small temporary emotions of the immediate present, the gratified vanity, the jealousy, the annoyance, the inevitable criticism. Even the gods that fight for Hellas are anonymous, save Zeus himself and —once only—the mail-clad Virgin of the Acropolis.[1]

With the Persians it is different. Persian names abound, and make a large element of colour in the piece. Persians are strange, far-off beings, exotic, and, if need be, heroic. There is no danger of bringing the action down to an everyday level by making the Elders ask the returning King:

> Why is Pharnouchos not with thee?
> And Ariomardos, where is he?
> Where is the Lord Seualkes gone?
> Lilaios where, the faithful son?
> Memphis, Tharybis and Masistras,
> And Artembar and Hystaichmas?
>   I ask these things.

Evidently the outlandish and sonorous names seemed to the contemporary Greeks, as they seem to us, far enough removed from the common to be suitable in tragedy. Aeschylus took pains over his Persian names. There are altogether fifty-five; forty-two of these are said by philologists to be

---

[1] Zeus 740, 762, 827; in exclamations 532, 915; Athena 347. (Pan is mentioned in passing, 449.)

genuine Iranian; ten are either of Greek form or somewhat transmuted by Greek analogy; only three have no visible etymology in Greek or Persian.[1]

Further, the Persians are treated in the heroic spirit. They are terrible men; full of pride, insatiable in their claims, and—as was natural in a practically monotheist nation—impious in their neglect of the gods. But there is no hatred of them; no remotest suggestion of what we now call 'war propaganda'. No Persian is in any way base: none is other than brave and chivalrous. The Elders are grave and fine; their grief is respected. Atossa is magnificent; not a word escapes her that is unworthy of a great Queen. Darius is a type of the old and good King, Father of his people. Xerxes himself, no doubt, as a contrast to Darius, has been wild and reckless, but even there the contrast is not between Persian and Greek; only between the Old King and the Young.

This greatness of spirit in Aeschylus' treatment of the enemy is remarkable. There is a similar fairness of judgement in Herodotus and of course in Thucydides. It was not a universal ancient convention, as we can see from the Old Testament or the history of Livy; or again by turning to the Persian dithyramb of Timotheos. But to read

---

[1] Keiper, *Die Perser des A. als Quelle für Persische Altertumskunde*, Erlangen, 1878.

the *Persae* during the Great War did indeed fill one with some shame at the contrast between ancient Hellas and modern Europe.

I have spoken before of the scene and the diction. The scene is merely the heart of Persia; the Greek poet does not care to be consistent about topography or to inquire exactly where the Council Chamber is situated with regard to the Tomb of Darius. It is not in the manner of ancient Greek art to trouble about such details. One may perhaps ask why the scene is not somewhere in Hellas among the victors who rejoice rather than the vanquished who lament: but the answer is simple. Aeschylus was producing a tragedy, a *Trauerspiel.* So the scene had to be among those who grieved, not those who rejoiced.

There is one point more which we may notice; the spirit in which the victory is to be taken and the moral to be drawn from it. It is the inevitable lesson of Greek tragedy, that pride leads to downfall. It is the moralizing of the processes of Nature; the Year waxes and then wanes: the corn and the vine reach their fullness and are then destroyed: man also grows great and then weakens and dies. Therefore let him walk humbly and not transgress.

The lesson is taught, in the first instance, at the expense of the Persians. They have not learnt the wisdom of Μηδὲν ἄγαν. They are conquerors on land from of old; now they must attack the

sea. They are masters of Asia; now they must
have Europe. In particular the Persians had committed one particular sin on which antiquity felt
strongly. They had destroyed temples and burned
images of the gods. Very likely they had partly
been moved by a spirit of conscientious monotheism; they had destroyed idols as Cromwell's
troopers destroyed church carvings; but to the
Greeks the act seemed to be mere wanton impiety.
The memory of it remained for centuries. Alex-
ander when he invaded Persia gave strict orders
that no sacred object whatever was to be injured,
and Polybius writing about 400 years after the
event still remembers what the Persians had done.

Why, then, after all their Hubris and sacrilege,
does one like the Persians and feel such sympathy
for them? It is partly that their names sound so
grand, partly that they all fight fairly and 'die
game'; but I think it is chiefly because Aeschylus
has steeped his verses in such charming colour
and made us believe it to be Persian. Whether
the colour is really Persian or only Lydian or
Phrygian is a question we need not wait to ask.
To Aeschylus and his audience the Persians were
the East, and it is the colour and music of the
East that he gives us. It came no doubt straight
from Phrynichus, of whose Sidonian songs we
have spoken before. The effect is produced
partly, as we saw above, by the use of strange
words with barbaric sounds; partly by a most

skilful handling of Ionian or oriental metres—
based on the foot described above (p. 69), two short
followed by two long, like 'by the grāve mound
of Atrīdēs' with a variant 'by the mound of great
Atrīdēs'—and the combination of them with
lyrical anapaests. There is no other play which
makes such use of the resolved anapaest with two
short syllables in place of the final long; or of a
metre which is really the ordinary anapaestic
dimeter minus the first foot.[1] Such technical
explanations can give little impression of the real
music in these lyrics, so frail, so delicate, which
has nevertheless preserved its magic for these two
thousand five hundred years.

When Aeschylus is challenged in the *Frogs*
to explain how precisely he has ennobled the
characters of his countrymen, Aristophanes makes
him answer that he has done so by the *Seven
against Thebes*. If the choice surprises a modern

---

[1] One may particularly notice the skilful transition from anapaests
to Ionics in ll. 65 ff., where ∪∪— stands repeatedly for ∪∪ — —, and
the peculiar beauty of the resolved anapaest

αἰνῶς αἰνῶς ἐπὶ γόνυ κέκλιται. (930)

πέμψω, πέμψω πολύδακρυν ἰαχάν. (940)

Cf. Mr. Yeats, 'The little flower I loved is broken in two', an effect
which is only possible in a milieu of extreme regularity. The anapaestic
dimeter *minus* the first foot gives a lingering effect:

> Ἰάνων γὰρ ἀπηύρα,
> Ἰάνων ναύφαρκτος
> Ἄρης ἑτεραλκής,
> νυχίαν πλάκα κερσάμενος
> δυσδαίμονά τ' ἀκτάν. (950 ff.)

reader, we may recollect that he could not well have cited the *Oresteia*; Clytemnestra is too near to the 'woman in love' motive which he contemptuously leaves to Euripides; the *Prometheus* has too much 'impiety' in it to serve the purpose; the *Supplices*, again, is all about women and the wrongs of women. Really, among our seven plays, none would serve Aristophanes' purpose except the *Seven against Thebes* and the *Persae*, which he mentions a few lines later.

Few modern readers would call the *Seven* their favourite Greek play, but it seems clear that the ancients admired it greatly. We must try to see why.

The trilogy of which it was part won the first prize in the year 467: *Laïus, Oedipus, Seven against Thebes*, followed by the satyr-play *Sphinx*. The Didascalia has come down to us in a more complete state than usual, and names the plays with which Aristias obtained the second prize and Polyphrasmon the third. The *Seven* was described by the orator Gorgias, in the phrase quoted above, as a Δρᾶμα Ἄρεως μεστόν, a *Drama brimming with Ares*, or the Spirit of War.[1] We are told that Telestes, the dancer used by Aeschylus, presumably as Leader of the Chorus, was such an artist that by his dancing in the *Seven against Thebes* he made the audience 'see the things that were being done'.[2]

---

[1] *Frogs*, 1021; Plut. p. 715E. [2] Ath. 22A.

Let us see if we can understand this criticism and this strong admiration.

The trilogy was evidently concerned with the Curse of the House of Laïus, by which the two sons of Oedipus must die childless and divide their kingdom by the sword.[1] The sons, Eteocles and Polynîces, agreed to reign alternately, a year at a time, but when Eteocles got the throne, he refused to yield it to Polynîces. (It is not clear which was the elder, nor yet whether Polynîces had in any special way shown himself unfit to be king.) Polynîces, being thus wronged, proceeded to commit the still greater wrong of collecting a foreign army and waging war against his native city.[2]

[1] Robert, *Oedipus*, i. 168 ff., 263 ff.; ii. 98. Hellanicus, fr. 12, says Polynîces gave up the kingdom, taking instead the χίτων (given by Athena) and ὅρμος (by Aphrodite) of Harmonia, and going to live abroad. Then Polynîces would be ὁ ἄδικος. But in Aeschylus, Polynîces claims Δίκη and Eteocles does not.

[2] The name Οἱ ἑπτὰ ἐπὶ Θήβας is as early as Aristophanes, but Verrall pointed out the curious fact that Aeschylus never uses the word Thebes or Theban, but always Καδμεῖα, Καδμεῖοι, Καδμογενεῖς. Nor does he ever mention the characteristic gods of Theban religion, Dionysus and Heracles, and has only one passing mention of the 'tomb of Amphion'. His Cadmeia is a sort of small Acropolis; the gates are close together. Tydeus at the first, Amphiaraus at the sixth, and Polynîces at the seventh are within speaking or shouting distance of each other. Possibly he thought of 'Thebes' as the more modern city that had spread round the old settlement of Cadmus. But here comes a still more puzzling feature. The Cadmeans speak 'the tongue of Hellas' (72) and observe the Hellenic customs (255); the invaders are a ἑτερόφωνος στρατός (155) and equip their horses βάρβαρον τρόπον (450). Cadmus was, of course, a Phoenician immigrant; it is hard to see how his people could be more 'Hellenic' than the Argives, unless,

In Euripides' *Phoenissae* there is a brilliant scene between the two brothers, in which the rights and wrongs of each are worked out. In Aeschylus we merely start the play with Eteocles King in Thebes defending his city against the invading army of Polynîces. The agreement, whatever it was, has failed, and the play would naturally be occupied with the fulfilment of the curse and the death of the two brothers.

But, as a matter of fact, for more than half the play the curse is, except for one line, practically ignored. The curse is put into the shade by an issue more thrilling. The scene is a besieged city, and the siege or capture of a city was to the ancient imagination a matter of overpowering interest. The city held all that was safe, all that was sacred. To have your city taken was the most terrible of fates; to take a city the most difficult of achievements. With no artillery, no heavy battering rams, no walls of circumvallation, there was nothing for it but to burn or batter in the gates or climb the walls with ladders. The odds were terrific against the invader getting inside, but woe to those inside if he did! The frescoes of Cnossus in pre-Hellenic days depict more than once an assault upon a city; so does the

indeed, as Verrall suggests, the word 'Hellas' is used specially of a district of north-western Greece, neighbouring the Homeric 'Hellas' but rather larger. There is much of the old Homeric tradition of which we have no knowledge because it was omitted in the final shape of the *Iliad* and *Odyssey*.

famous silver cup at Mycenae; so did the Shield
of Achilles in Homer and the Shield of Heracles
in Hesiod. The two most famous epics of Greece
are devoted one to the Siege of Thebes and the
other to the Siege of Troy. The horrors committed when Troy was taken form the subject of
at least two early Greek epics—the *Little Iliad*
and the *Iliu Persis*—and one great tragedy, the
Troades. The title πτολίπορθος, 'Sacker of
Cities', is noted by Cicero as the highest of hon-
ours; and as such is rejected by the Elders in the
Agamemnon, who pray 'May I never be a Sacker
of Cities!'[1] In the *Seven*, when the siege-motive
enters in, the curse-motive is almost forgotten.
We might have had Eteocles treated like Macbeth
in the fifth Act; a doomed and guilty man, tied
to a stake and unable to escape, but resolute to
'die game'. This figure is for a moment suggested
in Eteocles' last scene, but through most of the
play we have a picture quite different. We have a
Δρᾶμα Ἄρεως μεστόν, a beleaguered city and a
cool-headed heroic soldier defending it.

One reason, perhaps, why this play made such
an impression on contemporaries lay in its realism.
For a time Aeschylus stepped outside the circle
of legend to describe a thing—and a peculiarly
terrible thing—which might actually happen to
any member of his audience. The Chorus of the
play consists of terrified women. The women

[1] *Ad Fam.* x. 13. 2; *Ag.* 472.

know the attack is beginning, and rush from
their homes out into the street and then up to the
citadel, clinging to the images and altars of the
gods. They hear the shouts of the attacking party,
the thunder of horse-hooves. Nay, more, there
seems almost certainly to have been a whole
series of crashes and 'noises off'. The stage carpenter must have been kept busy. '*Do you hear
—or do you not—the clash of shields?*' cries one
woman. It would surely be fatal to ask the
question in that explicit form if there was no
sound to be heard. '*The noise terrifies me!*' cries
another: another hears spears striking at the gate
(100, 104). What particularly alarms them is the
Argive cavalry. There is the clang of the horses'
metal bits (123). Then the noise of chariots and
the scream of the wooden axles. (The axles of
ancient chariots were made of wood and wetted
with water instead of oil.) Then comes a crash
of heavy stones flung against the gate, and with
it again the clang of shields (152, 158; cf. 213 ff.
and 294).

It seems clear that Aeschylus during this chorus
tried to produce the actual noises of an assault
upon the gates, while his dancer Telestes made
people feel 'as if they saw the whole thing'. We
cannot but remember the various other ways in
which the stage-craft of Aeschylus showed itself
pre-classical and more ambitious than that of his
successors.

The next chorus, though almost equally realistic, seems to have dropped this particular effect of 'noises off' and concentrates on a description of what will happen if the besiegers conquer. The City itself—a city was almost a live thing to the Greeks—brought to death; the women dragged by their long hair as men drag horses; violations; robbery and murder; houses on fire; children crying; the mad wastefulness of the looting, the treasured possessions of a house flung out in the street and trampled on, and the housewife weeping with rage and humiliation. It is still, even by modern standards, a vivid and most 'real' picture.

There is much the same realism in the picture which Aeschylus draws of the internal condition of Thebes in its extreme peril. The women have got out of hand: they remind one of some of those crowds of terrified women that were sometimes seen during the air-raids on east London. They rush to the sacred images like a mob, not like an orderly Chorus. They speak severally. They interrupt each other. They scream. When Eteocles enters he falls upon them without mercy, scolds them into silence, and sends them down into the street away from the citadel and the images. Then, since it would be psychologically impossible for them to stay still, he wisely gives them something to do. Instead of demoralizing the town by lamentations, he bids them pull them-

selves together and go through the streets singing
an *ololugmos*—or cry of good omen—and informs
them of his vow, after the victory, to dedicate
spoils to a large number of gods on different
altars. That will give them something cheerful
to think about.

I imagine that this kind of scene was pretty
true to life as lived in a besieged city in antiquity.
But Aeschylus has added another element belonging to an age more savage and romantic than his
own. The champions who are attacking the City
are described as raging and boasting in a way
that belongs to pre-Hellenic or barbaric warfare,
but would have been out of place, and indeed
impossible, in a hoplite army of the fifth century.
They rage like Ares in Hesiod's *Aspis*, when he
tore round and round his *temenos* to work himself
up.[1] They boast as the Franks did in the Middle
Ages, and as some few Homeric heroes do, amid
the general disapproval. Aeschylus is not describing the warfare of his own day, but that of
the heroic age, when all life was wilder and fiercer.

But, just as Homer's true heroes never boast, as
his Greeks advance silently to battle while the
Trojans yell and scream, so Aeschylus' hero,
Eteocles, shows nothing but ἀνδρεία καὶ σωφροσύνη, the Fortitude and Self-control of the true
Hellenic soldier. His brother with a great army
of allies has come against the City. Eteocles is

---

[1] ὃς νῦν κεκληγὼς περιμαίνεται ἱερὸν ἄλσος, *Aspis*, 99. Cf. 61 ff.

apparently in the wrong—though of that we cannot be quite sure—he is certainly under the sway
of his father's curse. If the Curse holds, his
brother and he must die: and the expedition of
the Seven is in itself a proof that the Curse is
working. Meantime he has to defend his city and
keep up the general morale. He does it wonder-
fully well. Only once, for one moment, do we
catch a glimpse of his real state of mind. It is
when he is left quite alone, after the Scout has
gone and before the Chorus has arrived.

> O Zeus, O Mother Earth, O gods that keep
> Our wall! . . . O spirit of Evil, vast and deep,
> Sprung from my father's curse . . . I pray you, not
> My City! Tear not from the roots nor blot
> For ever out, in slavery and eclipse,
> A land that hath Greek speech upon her lips . . .

μή τοι πόλιν γε. We see that the Curse is on his
mind, and that he asks nothing for himself, only
for Thebes. Apart from this one flash of revelation, we see him only as a cool, capable leader of
men, always ready with a cheering word. The
ideal of a Ἔκτωρ, the 'holder' or 'upholder' of his
city against dangers and enemies, was strong in
the Greek mind from Homer's time onward, and
has provided the name of the principal defender
of Troy. Eteocles is a true 'upholder'. In the
opening scene he comes to the citadel with his
bodyguard and addresses the crowd of towns-
people who are too young or too old to be in the

regular army. He cheers them, inspires them, and sends them to the walls. The attack is coming; but all is prepared and they need not be afraid of the 'foreigners'. A Messenger or Scout comes, reports and departs. Eteocles goes to see to the wall. Then comes the rushing entry of the Chorus, and the next appearance of Eteocles is when he comes in anger and reduces the women to obedience in the way which we have described.

Then we have a series of scenes in which the Scout describes, one by one, the Argive chieftains at each of the Seven Gates, their raging boasts and the signs upon their shields. Eteocles with six chosen champions is prepared to meet them one by one; and has a cheerful retort to all their blazons. At the first gate is Tydeus with a figure of Night upon his shield, a central moon with stars shining round it. 'Good, let Night cover him, since he is asking for it.' Capaneus defies the thunderbolts of Zeus to keep him out of the City. 'Let us hope he will have the opportunity of meeting one.' The next assailant has the figure of a man scaling a city wall. 'Well, our champion will have two men and a city to carry home.' Hippomedon has the fiery monster Typhon on his shield. 'Excellent; we will send Hyperbios, who has Zeus on his. Zeus has always beaten Typhon.' Parthenopaios holds before him on his shield the Sphinx, the old enemy of Thebes. 'She will get such a thrashing, if she tries to come in here, that

she will turn and bite him!' At the sixth gate,
however, there is Amphiaraus, the righteous,
making no boast. That seems a harder case to
meet, but Eteocles is ready. 'A righteous man by
himself is formidable; but a righteous man con-
joined with the wicked perishes with them.' To
him goes the sixth champion and Eteocles is left
alone. At every point we have found him cool
and at his ease, ready-witted and concerned for
the morale of his people. 'But who is the seventh
Argive?' 'Your brother, Polynîces: on his shield
a figure of Justice and the words I RESTORE THE
RIGHT.' In a flash Eteocles is changed. His
coolness and self-control are gone. He is a des-
perate man, overmastered by the Curse.

O race god-maddened, god-abhorrèd, sown
   In endless tears, my father's and mine own . . .

'*I myself will go to meet him. King against King,
brother against brother, enemy against enemy.*' The
Chorus, formerly such feeble and frightened folk,
turn to calm him, to dissuade him from this awful
sin, the spilling of kindred blood. They address
him as τέκνον, 'My son'; so much have the rela-
tive positions changed! But he is firm. '*If disaster
must come, let it be disaster without shame. A man's
honour is the only thing that remains to him after
death.*' '*Calm yourself, my son, and think. Be cool
as you were but now,*' says the Leader. '*What is
the good? Apollo hates us. Better the whole race of
Laïus perish!*' The Leader pleads, but Eteocles

will not listen. '*My father's curse—the hate of him who should have loved me—hangs over these dry and tearless eyes, and whispers to me of one thing to gain* (κέρδος) *before death.*' The one thing to gain, of course, will be the slaying of his brother. So Eteocles goes out, to kill and to die. The race of Oedipus has perished and the City is saved.

In the last scene of lamentation over the two brothers, now united in death, an addition seems to have been made in our manuscripts, introducing the sisters Antigone and Ismene, and raising the question of the burial or non-burial of Polynîces; but Wilamowitz has convincingly shown that it cannot well be the work of Aeschylus. The discussion about Polynîces' burial is not quite consistent with the rest of the play, and the conception of the two sisters seems to be derived from the *Antigone* of Sophocles. In Aeschylus the curse is fulfilled: the race is wiped out, and the two brothers divide their inheritance equally, each having (908, 914) just land enough for a grave in his country's soil.

The play is no doubt rhetorical rather than dramatic. It is stiff in construction. Even in language, apart from its lyrics, it has not quite the same romantic beauty of diction as the *Persae* and the *Prometheus*. It is majestic and strong; and, if Gorgias was right in describing it as a 'drama brimming with the War-God', it certainly depicts him with rare imaginative insight. The dialogue is full of the splendour and heroism with which those particular people are facing their immediate ordeal, and which constitute the outside of war; the lyrics of the Chorus, impersonal and eternal, show the depths of horror and pity which are the essence of War itself, the abiding reality which lies deep below the justifications and excuses, the glories, vanities, and tragedies, of each particular quarrel.

It is worth noting that the *Seven* does not deal with its story as a great world-problem, as do all the other Aeschylean tragedies that have come down to us. If the play itself had been lost and we had only known the general story, we should have expected Aeschylus to treat the whole as a great issue between Δίκη and Εὐσέβεια—Justice and Piety. One could imagine long choruses in the style of the *Agamemnon*, explaining how every offence against Justice must inevitably bring its own punishment, so that Eteocles must suffer for his injustice to his brother, and his city suffer with him; and yet marvelling that any man, whether wronged or not, should be so blind as to commit the last impiety of making war against the land which gave him birth. In fact we have comparatively little said about this issue, though, of course, it may have been discussed in one of the earlier plays of the trilogy. We have here merely the vivid and unforgettable picture of the population of a besieged city, and one clearly outlined individual character, the doomed warrior, doing his duty to the last. Eteocles fits curiously well into Aristotle's famous description of the tragic hero: the noble character with the fatal flaw. He is clearly in his general nature one of those 'higher than ourselves' who are the suitable subjects of tragedy, but there is just one region—the hatred of his brother brought about by the Curse—in which he has neither wisdom nor justice nor self-control. Of the four cardinal virtues only Courage remains. He is, if I am not mistaken, the first clearly studied individual character in dramatic literature.

CHAPTER V

EVIDENCE OF THE FRAGMENTS

WE know the names of seventy-nine plays by Aeschylus, and there is some reason to suppose that he wrote ninety. Of these we have only seven preserved; and it is from those seven that we modern scholars try to draw conclusions about the whole artistic character of Aeschylus. The undertaking is risky but not impossible. Suppose that instead of possessing from the pen of Shakespeare thirty-eight plays *plus* four poems or sets of poems, we had only four plays: *Hamlet*, say, *Macbeth*, *Twelfth Night*, and *Richard II*; we should, I think, be able to form an idea of Shakespeare which would not be violently contradicted by the discovery of all the other plays.

To make the parallel more exact, however, we have to imagine that beside the four complete plays we had also before us something corresponding to the fragments of Aeschylus: one or two incomplete Shakespeare Birthday Books, for example, and a mutilated copy of Lamb's Tales and some books on different subjects which had occasion to quote or mention Shakespeare. We possess, after all, besides the seven complete plays about 460 or 470 'fragments' of Aeschylus; i.e. quotations of passages or lines or single words

from his plays, and many statements about them.[1]
We have also an ancient catalogue of his works
and a poor and fragmentary biography. It will
be useful to see whether the evidence, such as it
is, of these fragments corroborates or helps to
make clearer the conception of the poet which we
have drawn from the complete tragedies.

The first point that strikes a student of Aeschylus in Nauck's *Fragmenta Tragicorum* is the strong
Bacchic or Dionysiac element. This, of course, is
natural enough if tragedy was based on the ritual
of Dionysus and Aeschylus is our earliest trage-
dian. There are eleven plays directly on Dionysiac subjects: mostly on the regular 'propagandist
myth'—as Dr. Verrall has called it—of the Dionysiac religion, relating how the young god comes
to his own people and is rejected, and what vengeance falls on the wicked king who has made the
rejection. Normally this ought to be a *sparagmos*
or dismemberment, such as is suffered by Osiris
the Corn Sheaf, when the grain is scattered as
seed, and by the various other vegetation gods.
Thus the confusion, or identification, of the animal and vegetable worlds is responsible for many
of the ugliest features of primitive fertility rites.
Small animals were torn in pieces and scattered

---

[1] This collection is being increased year by year from the closer
examination of Egyptian papyri, but the passages recovered have so
far been very fragmentary. The useful little *Supplementum Aeschyleum*,
by H. J. Mette in Lietzmann's *Kleine Texte*, 1939, has already become
incomplete.

over the fields like seed; crops were encouraged
by phallic ceremonies. The *sparagmos* of human
beings, usually taboo priests or kings, seems actually to have occurred among Thracians and
other savage communities, and had a great effect
on the Greek imagination. When we first meet
it, it has become mystical, a symbol or instrument
of the Resurrection of the human body. The
vegetation gods are normally torn in fragments
that they may be reborn. Euripides' *Bacchae*
and Aeschylus' *Pentheus* tell how the god or
his representative is torn in pieces and scattered
over the fields; then, just outside the strictly
Dionysiac circle, we have a *sparagmos* of Orpheus,
Actaeon, Dirce, and others. We have also the
mystic death of the god's mother Semelê by fire
from Heaven, the subjugation of the Argonauts
by the first invention of wine in the *Kabeiroi*,
and so on.

Besides regular tragedies on Dionysiac subjects
we have a record of some fifteen satyr-plays, the
Chorus of which consisted of the half-divine, half-
brutish attendants of Dionysus. We are told by
Suidas that Aeschylus was regarded as the best
writer of satyr-plays ever known; second to him
came not either of the other two chief tragedians
but a much less celebrated playwright, Achaeus
of Eretria. The ancient critics seem always to
recognize that, while Dionysus was, of course,
the patron of all drama, there was something

specially Dionysiac about Aeschylus. Aristophanes (*Frogs*, 1259) calls him τὸν Βακχεῖον ἄνακτα, 'our Bacchic king'. Athenaeus and others say that he wrote his tragedies μεθύων, 'in a state of intoxication'. Obviously the phrase is figurative. Plutarch, in correcting the famous dictum of Gorgias, says that it is not so much that the *Seven against Thebes* is 'brimming with Ares', but that all Aeschylus' plays are 'brimming with Dionysus'.[1] This story is combined with the criticism of Sophocles upon his great predecessor: the more self-conscious artist observed that Aeschylus did the right thing but did not know what he was doing.[2] He wrote more from inspiration than from conscious art. One may add the tale from Pausanias, that when Aeschylus, as a child, was put in a field to watch the grapes and fell asleep, Dionysus appeared to him and commanded him to write tragedy. When he woke up he tried and found it quite easy.[3]

Thus we have evidence that Aeschylus wrote a large number of Dionysiac tragedies, and at least fifteen satyr-plays; he was considered the best writer of satyr-plays that had ever existed: he wrote in a state of Dionysiac inspiration, sometimes not with the clarity of a conscious artist. The picture is on the whole consistent. But let us consider more closely for a moment what a satyr-play was.

[1] Plut. Moralia p. 715 ᴇ   [2] Ath. x. 428 ꜰ   [3] Paus. i. 21. 2.

A satyr-play has, of course, nothing to do with our word satire. It was a peculiar form of drama, performed regularly at the end of a tragic trilogy, akin partly to tragedy and partly to comedy, in which the Chorus consisted of Satyrs. Its origin is unknown: I incline to the belief that originally, as tragedy represented the death of Dionysus or his counterpart, the satyr-play represented his triumphant return or resurrection at the head of his rout of attendant spirits. We have one complete satyr-play extant: the *Cyclops* of Euripides; about five hundred lines of another, the *Ichneutae* of Sophocles, and some fragments. We have also one pro-satyric play, a tragedy with a satyr-like element and a happy ending, performed in place of a satyr-play at the end of a tragic trilogy, Euripides' *Alcestis*. They all belong to a post-Aeschylean period, and the *Alcestis* may well represent a movement for getting rid of the primitive and uncivilized performance altogether. The satyr-play seems to have disappeared in the latter part of the fifth century, but was revived as a deliberate archaism in later times. It is a form of art so unlike anything now practised that we must devote a little time to considering it.

A satyr-play is set in the heroic world and deals with a traditional story. The Chorus consists of Satyrs, who are normally directed by old Silênus, the father of the Satyrs. The characters belong to the heroic world, but nearly always have something about them which is suited to comedy, or rather to κωμῳδία. We must remember that κῶμος means a revel, κωμικός means appertaining to a revel, and κωμῳδία is a revel-song. Thus the reveller Heracles in the *Alcestis* is typically a favourite character for satyr-plays; so is Hermes the baby cattle-stealer of Sophocles' *Ichneutae* or the Homeric *Hymn to Hermes*: so are Autolycus the prince of thieves, Odysseus who can play tricks on any giant, Thersîtes the scolder of princes, and Sisyphus who cheated Death. The Satyrs, whatever their origin, are to the Greek imagination something rather above men; they are Δαίμονες, daemons, immortal or at least gifted with immense ages of life, and possessed of strange superhuman wisdom, though as a rule they prefer not to remember it or think about it. At the same time they are wild creatures of the woods, with 'no more conscience than a squirrel', full of desires and delights unchecked by any inhibitions, drinking, playing, mocking, falling in love, running unashamedly away from danger. They are addressed as θῆρες, 'wild beasts', and are in fact part beast and part god. So is the satyr-play itself. It is partly heroic, written in the grand style and using even more boldly poetical diction than ordinary tragedy;[1] partly it is the sublimation of

---

[1] E.g. χείρεσσι and possibly γείνατο in *Alc.* 756, 839, and τως for ὡς *Ichn.* 39, 296. Anapaests are admitted more freely than in tragedy.

a drunken revel. The type to bear in mind is
Heracles in the *Alcestis*, not unfairly depicted in
Browning's *Balaustion*; the Heracles who is entertained in the mourning house of Admetus, not
knowing that Alcestis is just dead; who eats,
drinks, and sings, shocks the waiter by his tipsy
carousing, and then, when he learns the truth, is
suddenly sobered, goes forth into the night to
fight with Death and afterwards, with no rest, on
to further labours.

If we ask ourselves why the Athenians used,
and continued to use, such a strange art form, we
may remember that in the fifth century tragedy
and comedy were both unmixed. Tragedy was
in the tragic style and comedy in the comic;
tragedy dealt with 'beings greater than ourselves'
and comedy with beings 'lower'; there was no
form of drama which mixed them together until
the rise of the New Comedy in the fourth century.
The New Comedy dealt with average human
beings in private life, and mixed tragedy and
comedy as we find them mixed in our everyday
affairs. It was realistic, tender and humorous,
and it might be uninspired. Now the satyr-play
seems to have sought the mixture of tragedy and
comedy in a quite different way: not by observing
the average, but by realizing and combining the
heights and the depths. It saw Man as Pope
describes him in his famous Essay, 'a being darkly
wise and rudely great';

He hangs between in doubt to move or rest,
In doubt to deem himself a god or beast: . . .
Sole judge of truth through endless error hurled,
The glory, jest, and riddle, of the world.

It sees Man as a mystery, through the mist or the light of Dionysiac inspiration. And if Aeschylus was considered by ancient critics to have been the greatest writer of satyr-plays ever known, I think that, by combining that fragment of evidence with the evidence of the extant tragedies, we can get a most revealing glimpse into his mind. Here again he is the romantic or the mystic, fortunate in writing before the discreet limits of classical Attic tragedy had established themselves.

Such a suggestion is strikingly confirmed by another well-authenticated fragment of information about Aeschylus' life. There is an oft-repeated story that he was accused of revealing the mysteries.[1] He may or may not have been actually tried before a Court; some of our authorities say so: others speak only of a sort of riot in the Theatre, in which he might have been killed had he not fled for refuge to the Altar of Dionysus. The trouble seems to have been caused, as it naturally would be, not by one isolated offence but by some continuous tendency showing itself

---

[1] Ar. *Eth*. p. 1111 ᵃ 10 ἢ οὐκ εἰδέναι ὅτι ἀπόρρητα ἦν, ὥσπερ Αἰσχύλος τὰ μυστικά with *Schol*.; Aelian, *V.H.* v. 19 says he was tried for ἀσεβεία: before the Areopagus, says Clem. Alex. *Strom*. ii, p. 461. The riot in the theatre comes from Heraclides Ponticus in the Scholia to Aristotle.

in play after play. He was accused, says the Scholiast to Aristotle, of revealing the mysteries in the *Toxotides*, the *Priestesses, Sisyphus Petrokylistês, Iphigenîa*, and *Oedipus*: that is, in five different plays. (The *Toxotides*, or *Archer Maidens*, dealt with the *sparagmos* of the Dionysiac hero Actaeon; of the *Priestesses* nothing more is known; *Sisyphus Rolling the Stone* is so called to distinguish it from *Sisyphus the Runaway*, which was a satyr-play about the deceiving of Death. We cannot tell whether it was a satyr-play also or a tragedy. The *Iphigenîa* and the *Oedipus* were tragedies dealing with the well-known sagas.)

His defence, when accused of revealing the mysteries, was to prove that he did not know that the things he had said were ἀπόρρητα, or religious secrets; which is generally supposed to mean that he proved he had not been initiated. However that may be, it seems clear that for some reason or other he did strike his contemporaries as inclined in his Dionysiac inspiration to deal with deeper religious matters than they expected on the stage. He would grasp after the inner secrets of life, which the hierophants of the mysteries considered to be their own preserve. We have seen that in some of his extant plays he certainly did so.

One would like to know what a satyr-play or a Dionysiac tragedy was really like before the time of Aeschylus. The former developed into the pro-satyric *Alcestis*; the latter into the great mystic tragedy of the *Bacchae*. Those plays give us the end of the development; to form some idea of the beginning we can only use the suggestions of analogy and the few scattered fragments of evidence that come to us from Aristotle and others. We know from Aristotle that tragedy began in 'little myths and ridiculous diction'; that it was late in attaining σεμνότης, dignity or majesty; from Aristophanes, that it was Aeschylus first and chiefly who brought the *Semnotês* in.

The remains of his Dionysiac tragedies are very scanty. Of his *Bacchae* we have no trace except a name in a catalogue and a couplet warning against any breach of *Themis*, the sacred tribal custom. That is a characteristic sentiment of Euripides' *Bacchae*. *Semelê* or the *Water-carriers* dealt with Semelê's request to her divine lover that he should visit her in his full glory, and told how she died in the splendour of it. We are told that Semelê was represented as ἐνθεαζομένη, possessed by God; those who touched her body, in which the divine child was living, became filled with the spirit of prophecy.[1] There we have the Semnotês; the more primitive side is shown perhaps by the Water-carriers who formed the Chorus, seeking to put out the fire. Of the *Xantriai*, or *Carding Women*, we only know that they 'carded' or tore in strips the body of Pentheus on Mount Kithairon. The *Pentheus* must have told the same story, since

[1] Schol. Ap. Rhod. i. 636.

we find in the Argument to Euripides' *Bacchae* that it followed the same myth as that play. The *Nurses of Dionysus*—we may remember that he was brought up in secret, like Zeus, to save him from his Titanic enemies—seems to have been a satyr-play; we only know that the Nurses were rejuvenated or born again, a regular feature of the mystical religions and one which Euripides and Aristophanes repeat more than once.[1] The most numerous fragments come from the trilogy called *Lycurgeia*, consisting of the *Edônoi*, *Bassarai*, *Neaniskoi*, and the satyr-play *Lycurgus*. Lycurgus King of the Edônoi in Thrace was another Pentheus: he denied the god Dionysus, and smote his Nurses with an ox-goad, and therefore, as Homer says, 'was not for long on this earth'. He died by *sparagmos*, like Pentheus, though various particular versions of his dismemberment are current in later literature. (He was torn in pieces by horses or by panthers, or cut to pieces by himself in madness. He was imprisoned, like Orpheus and Rhesus, in the depths of Mt. Pangaion and worshipped afterwards.) In the second play, *Bassarai* or *Bassarides*, there was a Chorus of Maenads of the type called by that name, which is said to be a Thracian word for 'foxes'. They tore in pieces the prophet Orpheus, who neglected Dionysus and devoted himself to

[1] (Eur. *Bacch.* 183–90; *Hclid.* 849–5S; Ar. *Gêras, Amphiaraus, Knights*.)

the worship of Apollo or the Sun. The Chorus of the third play were νεανίσκοι. The word means merely 'Young Men', but is specially used of the initiates who have passed through the ordeals that transform a human being from Boy to Man. I suspect the *Neaniskoi* were really the Edônoi converted. It is not clear whether the trilogy consisted of three separate stories: the God's judgement on Lycurgus, the God's judgement on Orpheus, and a third which we do not know; or whether all three were occupied with the fate of Lycurgus, while taking in the fate of Orpheus as a digression. I think, however, that the first alternative is more probable, because we are told that in Aeschylus the fragments of the body of Orpheus were reassembled and buried by the Muses, an incident which seems like the final scene of the *Bassarai*.[1] One might compare the mourning of the Muse over her son in the *Rhesus*.

Names vary and incidents vary in this 'goat-song' or *Sacer Ludus* of Dionysus; but the essentials of the performance seem to be fixed. It was a sacred playing, or performance of the rites of the God, and it had certain fixed elements, which can be seen even in so late a production as the *Bacchae* of Euripides.[2] Several difficulties have been raised as to the plot of the *Bacchae* by critics who did not realize its profoundly ritual character.

---

[1] Eratosthenes, *Catast.* 24, p. 140.
[2] See Excursus in J. Harrison, *Themis*, pp. 341–60.

For example, the new God tells us that he is
coming for the first time through the world to
establish his worship, and that Thebes is the first
town in Hellas to be visited. Yet the Elders of
the Tribe, represented by Cadmus and Tiresias,
reproach Pentheus for not observing the ancient
customs and for setting himself up against 'the
traditions of his fathers, sanctions old as time'
(201 f.). The contradiction is manifest; but so is
the answer. It was a tradition and ancient custom
to welcome each year the new God who arrived
with the spring. Again, in most early statues and
paintings Dionysus is regularly a bearded figure,
whereas in the *Bacchae* Dionysus in his mortal
disguise is a beardless youth with long hair and a
girlish complexion, as beseems the embodiment
of the blossoming spring. Lastly, there is in the
Bacchae a supernatural earthquake which shatters
the house of Pentheus and sets free Dionysus,
who had been imprisoned in the stables. Yet, as
Dr. Verrall pointed out in a memorable essay, the
house seems to be in quite good condition afterwards, and people who come in later to see the
King do not seem to notice that anything odd
has happened to it. Here again, the explanation
lies in the traditional and ritual character of the
whole performance. It is an essential part of the
Dionysiac myth that when his minister is imprisoned, an earthquake is sent and the prison-
house broken. No doubt as theatrical technique

developed and audiences began to expect more realism, this earthquake began to be a difficulty, but it was firmly fixed in the story and could not be left out.

All these statements can be verified from the fragments of Aeschylus. In his *Bacchae* the offender is warned: 'Swift cometh evil among men, and most swift his sin returns to him who transgresseth Themis'; Themis is the ancient traditional custom. Again, in the *Edônoi* a line is preserved: ἐνθουσιᾷ Δὴ Δῶμα, βακχεύει στέγη, 'The house is possessed of God; the walls dance to Dionysus.' That is the earthquake. The house 'danced' at the appearance or epiphany of Dionysus, just like Pentheus' house in Euripides. Again, as to the dress and appearance of Dionysus himself, we have in the *Edônoi* a reference to a man 'who wears a tunic and Lydian fox-skin reaching to his feet', and we have a line addressed by Lycurgus to his prisoner Dionysus: 'Whence comes this woman-thing? (ὁ γύννις). What is his country? What his dress?' The Aeschylean Dionysus therefore must have presented just the same appearance as the Dionysus of Euripides, have been imprisoned by the hostile King in the same way, caused the same earthquake, and been addressed in much the same language.

The best parallel to this Dionysiac *Sacer Ludus* is without doubt to be found in the liturgical plays of the Middle Ages, plays representing the

Massacre of the Innocents, or Noah and the Flood, or the story of Balaam. The play might be little more than a division of the liturgy into parts among the monks inside the cathedral; it might be a play based on the liturgy but performed outside and using plenty of new dialogue and new characters. It might consist of 'little stories and ridiculous diction', like some of the Noah plays, or it might rise to the sublimity of the Passion-play at Oberammergau.[1] But in each case, whatever new poet or producer might take the work in hand, the main elements were firmly fixed in the tradition and could not be changed.

Rich materials for drama lay before these sacred dramatists of the Middle Ages: comic scenes between Balaam and his ass, in which the ass gets the best of the argument: comic scenes in which Noah gets drunk and the Almighty regrets having gone to so much trouble in saving him: comic scenes between Mary Magdalen *in gaudio*, before her repentance, and the *unguentarius* from whom she bought her cosmetics: and on the other hand, the germs of great ideas and moments of spiritual anguish; the Passion itself, the repentance of the Magdalen, or the cry of the Angel to the murdered innocents: *Vos qui in pulvere iacetis, expergiscimini et clamate*. Something similar must have lain before Aeschylus when he sat down to his satyr-plays or his Dionysiac tragedies. It was

---

[1] See E. K. Chambers, *The Mediaeval Stage*, vol. ii, chap. xix.

the essence of his genius that he saw beyond all
the trivialities and drunken antics of his raw
material the essential mystery of Life and Death
and the essential greatness of soul with which
Man, at his best, faces and even conquers it.

Of course he was laughed at. In one tragedy,
the *Kabeiroi*, of which we know almost nothing
except that it must have been concerned with the
mysteries belonging to those daemons, he introduced the Argonauts μεθύοντας, in a state of
intoxication. The visit of the Argonauts to Lemnos is connected with stories of the first planting
or discovery of the vine, and it seems likely that
he showed the effect of the mysterious drink when
tasted for the first time by Man. It was a possible
scene but risky; one is reminded of the scene in the
Bacchae (178–209) where the old men Cadmus
and Tiresias are suddenly filled with mysterious
strength, so that they dance to the God. But that
scene is carefully and tactfully written. Aeschylus
was less cautious; and it seems that the Comic
poet Crates, having seen the *Kabeiroi*, proceeded
to write a parody, with men more realistically
drunken, in his play *Geitones, The Neighbours.*

It would be extraordinarily interesting to know
how Aeschylus really expounded the great Dionysiac myth. In the *Bacchae* of Euripides, the one
instance where we find that myth treated with
tense imagination and feeling by a poet of genius,
almost all critics feel the presence of a riddle

though they are not yet agreed upon the answer.
That the *Bacchae* means something; that it is not
merely an exciting and rather revolting story put
on the stage with a decoration of fine words, is
the conviction of almost all who have studied it.
That the Bacchanals of the Chorus are things of
beauty and their songs wonderful poetry seems
undeniable; that the God himself is cruel and
inhuman and is felt to be so even by his worshippers seems almost equally clear. But to say so
much is to state the problem, not to answer it.
The play cannot be a mere denunciation of the
Dionysiac religion; it cannot be a mere reversion
to extreme superstition on the part of a veteran
champion of free thought. I have explained my
own views elsewhere.[1] One wonders greatly what
Aeschylus made of the same material and the same
problem in his repeated treatments of it. But there
is no evidence to guide our conjectures. He did
raise the Bacchic drama from triviality to serious
greatness; he did so by seeing the mystery lying
behind it. Of that we can be sure, but of little more.

There was also another method by which he
raised the whole dignity of drama and deepened
its seriousness. We are told by Athenaeus that
Aeschylus described his tragedies as 'slices from
the great banquets of Homer',[2] and the saying is

---

[1] *Euripides and his Age*, in the Home University Library, pp. 181–9.
[2] τεμάχη τῶν Ὁμήρου μεγάλων Δείπνων Ath. viii. 347E. Cf.
Wilamowitz, *Herakles*, i. 94. 59.

often repeated by modern writers without much attempt to analyse its meaning. To understand it we should first remember that in Aeschylus' day the word 'Homer' covered the whole mass of heroic legend, not merely the *Iliad* and *Odyssey*; and next we should notice the subjects on which the predecessors of Aeschylus mostly framed their tragedies. The predecessors were Thespis, Choeri- lus, Pratinas, and Phrynichus. We know the names of four tragedies attributed to Thespis; they are of doubtful authenticity, but, if genuine, they all belong to the Dionysiac or Year-Daemon type of subject. Pratinas introduced the satyr- play into Athens, and thirty-two of his fifty dramas were satyr-plays. Choerilus made some innovations in the treatment of choric dances and some improvements in costume; otherwise he is chiefly known by the proverb 'When Choerilus was a king among satyrs'. So far, tragedy seems to be confined to the circle of Dionysus and the satyrs, and the 'little myths' of what Dr. Leaf used to call 'field magic'. A change begins with Phrynichus, from whom Aeschylus learnt so much. His subjects still seem mostly to have belonged to the Dionysiac or satyric group: Actaeon with his *sparagmos*: *Alcestis*, which was a satyr-play; *Tantalus*, usually a satyr-play sub- ject; the *Danaïdes*, probably treated in the pre- Aeschylean mocking style which we find in Pindar's version. Yet Phrynichus did, apparently,

try to find subjects more worthy of that fine
Ionian music of his and those dances, with movements 'many as the waves of the sea in storm',[1] and
thus to impart to them a new dignity or *Semnotês*.
In his *Women of Pleuron* he made the bold experiment of treating one epic subject, the death of
Meleager; and in two other plays he used subjects
of the kind that we should call historical. The
first of these, the *Capture of Miletus*, not only
involved him in public trouble and a fine of a
thousand drachmae; the authorities also prohi-
bited any dramatist from making a tragedy out
of that subject in future. Herodotus (vi. 21)
attributes this prohibition to the soreness of the
Athenian public over the capture of Miletus,
accentuated perhaps by some pricks of conscience
about their own inaction. But it may have been
due to a religious or artistic feeling that the *Sacer
Ludus* of Dionysus was not the occasion for treating contemporary politics. If so, the feeling had
perhaps changed by the time he produced his
second tragedy on a contemporary subject, the
Persae; or again it may be that this particular
subject, though in date contemporary, was recognized as belonging by right of quality to the
heroic age. However, for our present purpose,
the point is that Phrynichus did enlarge the scope
of tragedy and make it less trivial by including
two subjects from recent history, and one, if not

---

[1] Plutarch, *Moralia*, p. 732 F.

several, from the epic saga. He cut at least one 'slice from the great banquets of Homer'. Aeschylus went much farther; he took subject after subject from the epic tradition, and thereby put tragedy on the same high level as the epic itself.

The two great poems which were recited every four years at the Panathenaea in Athens and which began about this time to be taught to boys and young men as the staple of a literary education were distinguished from the other poetry before and around them by one quality above all others: their *Semnotês*, dignity, magnificence. The *Iliad* and *Odyssey*, by their very perfection as compared with the masses of old traditional verse from which they were carved, exercised an immense influence upon Greek poetry, both for inspiration and for destruction. The Lesbian school indeed had its own perfection; parts of Sappho and Alcaeus are unaffected by Homer, parts show a power of absorbing him without loss of their own individuality. But of the poetry composed on the mainland scarcely anything remains which has not been largely shaped by this new Homeric influence. The almost complete disappearance of the vast volume of epic poetry which was not selected for the recitation; the similar disappearance of Stesichorus in spite of his efforts to 'Homericize' his lyrical stories; the evidences of a similar effort in the remains of Hesiod; the accidental survival of two poems by Corinna, showing us

what the native poetry must have been like in
Boeotia when indifferent to Homeric influences—
all these phenomena point to the same conclusion.
And it may be that when Aeschylus spoke of the
'great banquets of Homer' he was thinking not
merely of the epic subjects in general but of the
grand style which he had learnt to admire at
the Panathenaea and which he introduced to the
Dionysia. Certainly, though he chose his subjects from the whole realm of epic tradition, his
diction had the special artistry of the *Iliad* and
Odyssey and achieved the same greatness of utterance. The 'little myths and ridiculous language'
disappeared for ever, and tragedy took the heroic
saga and the 'grand style' for her own.

Only once did Aeschylus form a tragic trilogy
out of the main story of the Homeric poems as
we know them: the *Myrmidons*, the *Nereids*, and
the *Phrygians* or *Hector's Ransom* treated the same
theme as the *Iliad* itself.[1] The experiment was
not repeated. The tragedians, while roaming
freely over the field of epic saga, kept carefully
away from the main story of the *Iliad* and *Odyssey*.
These two subjects definitely belonged to the
Festival of Apollo at the Panathenaea; they were
recited in the proper Apolline manner. But the
rest of 'Homer'—to use the word in its ancient
fifth-century sense—was not appropriated to any
particular performance or recitation and was at

[1] See *Rise of the Greek Epic*, chap. xii (p. 297 in ed. 4).

the disposal of Dionysus if he wanted it. At any rate, we find as a matter of fact a division carefully maintained. The *Iliad* and *Odyssey* are recited at the Panathenaea; the rest of the heroic saga is open to be treated at the Great Dionysia in the form of tragedy. The trilogy we have just mentioned is the sole exception. It embraces a fine tragic subject and one peculiarly tempting to Aeschylus. The opening of the *Myrmidons* is preserved. 'Great Achilles, seest thou this? The Greeks labouring and broken beneath the spear....' It is the appeal of his own soldiers to Achilles to save the Greeks and not stay aloof because of the slight done to his honour by Agamemnon. We know that in Aeschylus he sat silent a long time, deigning no answer; that at last he yielded so far as to let Patroclus and the Myrmidons go to battle while he himself still refused. Without him, venturing too far, Patroclus was killed by Hector. In the next play the Nereids, sisters of his mother Thetis, come to comfort Achilles for the death of his friend and bring him new celestial armour. Thetis warns him that the death of Hector will be followed quickly by his own, and in that knowledge he goes out to avenge his friend. He will slay Hector; he will give him no burial; he will give his body to the dogs to eat. He will spare no detail of the uttermost vengeance lest he should seem to be thinking of his own fate and using his friend's honour as a bargaining point in order to gain mercy or burial for himself. In the third play Aeschylus treated the great tragic scene of *Iliad* xxiv; the visit of old Priam to the Greek camp to beg Achilles to give back the body of Hector for burial; Achilles' fury, his pity, his burst of tears, and the two enemies weeping together and reconciled by their common misery. Magnificent as that scene is in Homer, one wonders if it may not have been even more full of drama and philosophic depth in the hands of Aeschylus.

A few tragedies indeed were based on incidents mentioned by the way in the *Iliad* or *Odyssey*. The *Oresteia*, for instance, centres in the slaying of Agamemnon, which is mentioned three times in the course of digressions in the *Odyssey*; and it is worth noticing that, while Aeschylus treats the whole subject in a different spirit, far more tragic and intense and searching, he keeps some details which show that he had passages from the *Odyssey* in his mind.[1] The *Psychostasia*, or *Soul-Weighing*, again, is based on a motive which also occurs in the *Iliad*. There, before the last duel, Zeus takes a balance and lays in the scales of it two dooms of Death, one for Achilles and one for horse-taming Hector. He lifted the balance, and

---

[1] For example, the Watcher at the beginning of the *Agamemnon*; cf. *Odyssey*, λ. 520 ff.; the long explanation of Menelaus' absence, *Ag.* 617–80, cf. *Od.* γ. 249–312; and even the use of one or two peculiar words, such as βάλλω, intransitive, *Ag.* 1172, cf. *Od.* λ. 424.

the doom of Hector turned the scale. (*Il.* X. 209.)
So Apollo deserted him, and he was slain. In
Aeschylus it is a weighing of lives, not of dooms,
and the two warriors are not Achilles and Hector
but Achilles and Memnon; but, what is more important, in the scene where Zeus lifts the scales,
the mothers of the two champions are present,
Thetis and Eos, both beautiful, both divine, both
in anguish, each praying with equal right for the
life of her own son. That is tragedy; that turns
the epic story into a world issue. There was also
a play called *Penelope* of which we know little,
except a line in which the disguised Odysseus
seems to be saying that he is a stranger from Crete.
If it was a satyr-play, as seems likely, there was
no objection to satyr-plays caricaturing the Apolline epic at the Dionysia. (Cf. the *Cyclops* and
Sophocles' *Nausicaa*.)

Most, however, of the 'slices' which Aeschylus
cut from the great banquets of Homer had no
connexion with the *Iliad* or *Odyssey*. The trilogy
to which the *Seven against Thebes* belonged, *Laïus*,
Oedipus, and *Seven*, came from the Theban cycle
of legends. Another dealing with the death of
Ajax came from other parts of the Trojan group.
The *Award of the Arms* treated the contest of
Ajax and Odysseus for the arms of Achilles, and
the defeat of Ajax. The next play gave that hero's
madness and death; it was called *The Thracian
Women*, from the captives of Ajax who formed the

Chorus, and perhaps suggested to Sophocles the beautiful character of the captive Tecmessa in his *Ajax*. The third play, *The Women of Salamis*, probably dealt with the situation described in Sophocles' *Ajax* (1006–20): the return of the noble bastard Teucer to Salamis without his brother, his telling of the story to Telamon, the broken-hearted Telamon's curse, and Teucer's flight across the sea to build another Salamis in unknown lands.

There must have been a trilogy on the legend of Perseus; first *The Net-drawers*, who pulled up from the sea Danaë with her baby child: then some play about Perseus' exploits; then the *Polydectes*, telling how Perseus, long supposed to be dead, returned in time to save his mother from that tyrant. Of other plays we know singly. The *Mysians* told how Telephus, wounded by the fatal spear of Achilles, and learning through an oracle that only 'he who hurt shall heal'—ὁ τρώσας ἰάσεται—made his way back from Tegea to Mysia to make supplication to his enemy. He either was, or pretended to be, under a stain of blood-guilt; and therefore had to make the journey without speaking. One may conjecture that he approached Achilles as a stranger praying for purification, and then, when Achilles accepted him, revealed his name and his purpose. The play served as a model to Euripides in his celebrated *Telephus*, the occasion of so much wit in Aristophanes. There were plays on *Palamedes*,

the true wise man, wrongly condemned on the
evidence of the false wise man, Odysseus; on
Niobe and the cruel god who had professed to be
her friend and slew her children; on *Philoctêtes*,
deserted by the Greeks at Lemnos and now indis-
pensable to the success of their arms; on *Iphigenîa*,
sacrificed or miraculously saved. On the borders
between epic and mere Year-Daemon ritual we
seem to find the curious trilogy which contained
the *Hypsipyle* and the *Nemea*, and treated of the
sequel to the ghastly deed done by the women of
Lemnos. Barbarian or Pelasgian women they
must have been, whose island had been taken from
them by the Greek invaders, and all their men
slain. The women were enslaved and taken as
concubines; but somehow they were trusted too
soon, and rose secretly and killed every Greek
man in the island. Then, left alone, in imminent
danger, they were visited by the Argo on its
voyage after the Golden Fleece. Naturally they
would not let the Argonauts land till they made a
treaty of peace, and agreed to live with them and
be their 'men'. That came in the first play,
Hypsipyle. In the third, the princess Hypsipyle
seems to have been a slave at Nemea near the
Isthmus of Corinth. The Nemean Games were
founded in honour of her child or nursling Arche-
morus, who was killed by a mysterious snake.

We seem to see tragedy in the hands of Phrynichus and Aeschylus trying to escape from its

original sphere of 'little myths and ridiculous language' and find some higher and wider territory. It deepens the meaning of its Dionysiac *molpê*, but that becomes monotonous. It tries subjects of contemporary history, but that leads to trouble. It trespasses on the story of the *Iliad* and *Odyssey*, but that is Apollo's domain and Dionysus is warned off. It finally takes possession of all the vast field of heroic saga that is not recited at the Panathenaea and the innumerable local myths that are capable of being raised to a heroic level.

There is one further point which is of cardinal importance for the appreciation of Aeschylus, but which cannot be made clear to English readers without detailed linguistic study; viz. the majestic diction, the ῥήματα σεμνά, flowing over at times into the use of strange and difficult phrases. The fragments entirely bear out the evidence of the complete tragedies: one could scarcely mistake the author of the lines from the *Niobe* (fr. 161):

Μόνος θεῶν γὰρ θάνατος οὐ Δώρων ἐρᾷ,
οὐΔ᾽ ἄν τι θύων οὐΔ᾽ ἐπισπένΔων ἄνοις·
οὐΔ᾽ ἔστι βωμὸς οὐΔὲ παιωνίζεται,
μόνου Δὲ Πειθὼ Δαιμόνων ἀποστατεῖ.

But on this point we may safely accept without further examination the verdict of Aristophanes. In the contest between Euripides and Aeschylus in the *Frogs*, one subject after another is taken: general style, moral influence, prologues, lyrics, are all passed in review; and no decision can be made, the two rivals are so equal in merit. Then at last it is decided to weigh the verses of both in the balance, and when it comes to that, Aeschylus wins every time hands down. When a Greek scholar nowadays asks himself why exactly it is that he finds Aeschylus in some way greater than other poets, the reason that emerges will, I think, generally be this tremendous majesty of diction. It seems indeed a 'large utterance of the early gods'.

It was proposed at the beginning of this book to show how Aeschylus became the creator of tragedy by three main achievements: he made tragedy *Semnon*, a thing of majesty: he was a pioneer in stage technique, making experiments too bold for the more classic writers who followed him; and lastly, he was a poet of great ideas, who found in the saga not merely the material for ingenious or exciting or moving stories but for great problems of the sort which can perhaps never be solved, and must be contemplated by emotion as much as by philosophy.

In the extant plays we found that this last contention can be clearly substantiated. In the *Prometheus* we have the world problem of Job, the 'great argument' which Milton also vainly attempts. In the *Supplices* what one may roughly call the mystery of sex, the sacredness of virginity, so strongly felt by the ancients, combined with

the equal sacredness of love; in the *Persae* perhaps
little beyond the eternal problem of Hubris and
its requital; in the *Seven* the conflict between
Dikê and Eusebeia, between strict justice and that
devotion surpassing justice which a man owes to
his gods, his mother, or his city. In the *Oresteia*,
as we shall see, there is the greatest problem of all,
the eternal chain of Justice or Retribution for
wrong done, set against not merely the necessity
but the duty of Forgiveness, and its attempted
solution through making the ruling principle of
the universe not a system of physical causation
but a living and free Mind. In the disjointed
fragments which are all that remain of the great
majority of Aeschylus' plays it is, of course, hard
to find a connecting purpose or plan. The Bacchic
tragedies, like the *Lycurgeia*, must presumably
have raised that problem which is so vividly
present in the *Bacchae* of Euripides.[1] It is a problem with many facets. One of them is, roughly,
the conflict between the claims of the sober and
the inspired elements in life: the 'crowded hour
of glorious life' with all its possibly ruinous consequences balanced against the 'age without a name',
with its comparative safety and innocence; the call
of ecstasy against that of duty or prudence.

Elsewhere among the fragmentary plays we
seem to find suggestions of similar conflicts of
ideas. We have already noticed how the Soul-

---

[1] See above, p. 160.

weighing, which in Homer is merely an impressive incident, is developed by Aeschylus into the old and well-known problem raised by every war: the prayers of the good people on each side for the help of the same god against the good people on the other side. In a similar way, the death of Sarpêdon before Troy and the carrying of his body by the two spirits, Sleep and Death, to burial in his own country Lycia, is treated as a direct narrative in the *Iliad*: in Aeschylus' *Europa* it was all seen through the eyes of the dead soldier's mother, Europa, in her own home far away from the battle. One of the epic trilogies has its moral conflict already provided in the Homeric story, the conflict in Achilles between personal honour and loyalty to his chief, and again between stubborn pride and σωφροσύνη, finally between a storm of passions based on his deep love for the friend whose death he has caused and the claims of what the Greeks would have called Αἰδώς or Εὐσέβεια, Ruth or Piety. The conflict in the *Award of the Arms* is not very different; on the one hand, the hero's passionate sense of slighted honour, leading to madness and disloyalty and repentance; on the other, the *Aidôs* that is shown by Teucer and perhaps, as in Sophocles, by Odysseus, and sinned against by Ajax himself, and by Telamon. Of the *Philoctêtes* of Aeschylus we know little, except an account of the opening given by Dio Chrysostom (lii). Dio compares

the three plays on Philoctêtes by the three
tragedians respectively, and expresses the greatest
admiration for the majesty and simplicity of
Aeschylus. His very lack of ingenuity goes well
with a heroic atmosphere. Dio does not tell us
whether the general treatment of the play was
the same as in Sophocles, though he implies that
it was. If so, the point is interesting. Sophocles'
Philoctêtes is a psychological drama. Philoctêtes,
wounded with a poisonous wound, had been left
behind at Lemnos by the Greeks acting under
the advice of Odysseus. After nine years they
learn from an oracle that Troy can only be taken
by him and his arrows. Odysseus undertakes to
try to fetch the wronged and angry man to Troy,
but, since he is known to Philoctêtes as an old
enemy, takes with him the young and chivalrous
Neoptolemus, son of Achilles, whom Philoctêtes
has never seen. Under Odysseus' orders the young
man worms himself into the sick man's confidence, and gets possession of the bow and arrows;
then, when he has got them, is disgusted at his
own treachery, breaks down, gives back the bow,
defies Odysseus, and is ready to suffer whatever
may come to him rather than profit by so base a
lie. Sophocles seems to have introduced the character of Neoptolemus, and it is possible that it was
he who gave this special psychological turn to a
story which was merely epic before. Yet I do not
think it likely. There is no real solution to the

problem of getting Philoctetes' help unless he can be induced to come willingly. The Odysseus of Aeschylus must, I think, not only have come to Philoctetes unrecognized in the first instance, but must in the end have revealed himself and actually won his old enemy's forgiveness. That was a difficult theme; but Dio tells us that Aeschylus' play was criticized as having a difficult theme and not inventing any devices to make it probable, whereas his successors invented several. It is worth remembering that at least two of Aeschylus' known trilogies end with a reconciliation of enemies.

It may seem to some readers that these issues of justice and forgiveness, of virginity and love, honour and loyalty, are too modern and civilized for an early Greek poet; but I think that would be a mistake. My statement is perhaps put in modern terms; but the conflicts themselves have constantly been present in human society even in its primitive stages. It matters greatly to a savage army whether a particular chief will stand out for his own honour or sink it in the common welfare; to a savage woman to find how she can observe her religious taboos and yet meet her lover; to a primitive avenger of blood how far the reciprocal slaying must continue and whether there is ever to be peace for him and his children. The conflicts are permanent enough; so far from creating them, civilization has probably softened them.

Another difficulty may cause more just misgiving. One cannot but wonder how far it is really possible for a modern Englishman, separated from the Greek poet by more than two thousand years of history, as well as great gulfs of thought, language, and social structure, to penetrate with any intimate understanding into the mind of Aeschylus. It may be that we Greek scholars are merely deluding ourselves. Even after years of close and loving study, is such understanding as we seek to acquire really possible? I hardly dare assert an affirmative; we are always misunderstanding our intimate friends; yet I think we should be cautious before committing ourselves to a definitely negative answer. We do enjoy Greek poetry. That is a plain fact. We do somehow appreciate and enjoy various extremely subtle elements in it—little waves of rhythm in a language which—I admit—we do not know how to pronounce; the use of a dialectic form, of a phrase with particular associations; even, I think, on rare occasions the use of a word of which the meaning is not certainly known. The communication of beauty, if that is the right word, is a more subtle and mysterious process than our psychologists have yet analysed, and I am inclined to suspect that many people now living have had closer and more intimate communion with the thoughts of Shakespeare, or Dante or Virgil or, it may be, Aeschylus, than with those of their next-door neighbours.

CHAPTER VI

THE *ORESTEIA*

HE first thing that strikes a reader who
turns from Aeschylus' earlier plays to the
Oresteia is the increase of active drama. In the
earlier plays there is one great situation, in which
the poet steeps our minds, with at most one or two
sudden flashes of action passing over it. Woman
pursued by the lust of unloved man, the Saviour
of mankind nailed eternally to the rock, the suspense of a great people expecting and receiving
the news of defeat in war, the agony of a besieged
city—these are all the kind of subject that might
be treated in a simple choral dance with nothing
but words and music. At most Aeschylus, transforming the *Molpê* into drama, adds a brief flash
of action: in the *Supplices* the rescue of the women,
in the *Prometheus* the binding in the prologue and
the casting into Hell at the end, in the *Seven*
the scene where Eteocles goes out to kill his
brother and to die. In the *Persae* there is a steady
tension throughout, diversified by the entrance of
the Messenger, the evocation of Darius, and the
entry of Xerxes, but the situation is never changed,
only seen from different angles.

In the *Oresteia*, on the other hand, we have a
real story in which the action is strong and pro-
gressive; we have a plot culminating in murder, a

vengeance, and a trial. Yet if any one begins to
treat the *Oresteia* as a mere plot-drama of the
ordinary modern type, or even of the same type
as the *Oedipus Tyrannus*, he will find that somehow it goes wrong. If he wants action he will be
worried by the interminable delays, choruses,
theological discussions; if he boldly cuts these out
and starts where the action begins, he will find he
has got nothing but an unpleasant melodrama.
Even Aristophanes complained of the 'long song-
systems, four on end' with which Aeschylus dosed
his audience (*Frogs* 914 f.); the first Chorus of the
Agamemnon is 211 lines long; yet the truth is that
for the proper understanding of the *Oresteia* not
one strophe of Chorus can be left out.

There is all the difference in the world between
a story of adventure and a dramatic poem, between a play by Dumas the elder and a play by
Tolstoy. In the former you take for granted what
a murder is or, let us say, what a lover or a husband
is; and you spend your ingenuity in making an
exciting story about lovers, husbands, and mur-
ders; in the latter you take for granted some
story and spend your imagination in trying to
realize what a murder is, or what it really means
to be a husband or a lover. In the *Oresteia* it is
taken as known that Agamemnon conquered
Troy, having sacrificed his daughter Iphigenîa in
order to do so, that his wife Clytemnestra murdered him, and that her son Orestes murdered or

executed her and went mad in consequence. The
effort of the drama is to make us feel what it is
to take a city, to sacrifice a daughter, to hate a
husband so much as to kill him, or to feel driven
to an act so horrible as the slaying of one's
mother. And, observe, it is not a mere effort of
imaginative psychology: that would give us a play
like Zola's *Thérèse Raquin* or perhaps Dostoiev-
sky's *Crime and Punishment*. It might be rather
sordid. The effect here is, as it were, to pierce
into the ultimate meaning of these ghastly and
incredible disturbances of the cosmos of life.
There is religion in it as well as psychology, and,
above all, there is poetry. I would almost say that
a reader who has really steeped himself in the
Oresteia would feel what poetry is, would feel
what religion is, and would know a surprising
amount about the human heart, at any rate in its
greater and more tragic aspects. That may be
wrongly expressed; but it is some impression of
that sort which makes many Greek scholars feel
inclined to say, with Swinburne, that the *Oresteia*
is perhaps 'the greatest achievement of the human
mind'.

The amount of preparation before the action
begins is very great: we have to wait till line
800, about half through the play, before Agamemnon enters, and till 970 before he enters the
house. Up to there it is all atmosphere and suspense. Then, except for a negative effect at 1033

where we expect a death-cry and have instead a
further entrance of Clytemnestra, there is again
atmosphere and suspense until Cassandra enters
the house at line 1330. Then in the last three
hundred lines of the play come the death-cry of
Agamemnon, the discovery of Clytemnestra with
the dead bodies of her husband and Cassandra,
the conflict between her and the Elders, the
triumphant entry of Aigisthos, and the beating
down of all opposition.

In the *Choëphoroe*, the second play of the trilogy, the proportions are extremely different. It
is the only play by Aeschylus which depends at
all largely for its effect on plot and action. The
atmosphere and the moral issues have been so
fully prepared in the *Agamemnon* that in this play
the action can begin at once. As soon as we see a
young armed man standing in prayer at a neglected tomb we know what the situation is. And
when Clytemnestra makes an unannounced and
unexpected entrance, and we see her standing,
grave and courteous, exactly where she stood, a
short time back, in mad exultation over the dead
bodies of Agamemnon and Cassandra, we need
no explanations or reflections to make us feel the
atmosphere. There is only one scene which would
seem to a modern eye to delay the action unduly,
viz. the prayer of Orestes and Electra at Agamemnon's tomb, which occupies 200 lines, or about a
fifth of the play. Apart from that one scene the

action is as rapid as that of the *Oedipus*: and that
scene is absolutely cardinal to the plot, and every
line of it necessary. Orestes is discovered alone at
the grave; he sees the Libation-bearers approach,
and hides himself. He discovers from Electra's
prayer who they are, and how strange a purpose
has brought them there—the murderess, frightened by a dream, has actually sent prayers and
libations to her victim in the grave. He reveals
himself and is recognized. The brother and sister
kneel, passionately praying to their father to awake
and help them; they cry and cry to him till at last
they know in their hearts that their prayer is
heard. Agamemnon has awakened. The dead
are with them and they need have no fear. Orestes
disguises himself, and returns to knock on the
Palace Door asking for Aigisthos. Instead there
comes his mother; this makes his task harder, but
he tells glibly the story of his own death and is
welcomed in. Presently his old Nurse comes out
in tears; she has heard the news of Orestes' death,
and has been sent by Clytemnestra to inform
Aigisthos, who is abroad. He is to come at once.
'Is he to bring his body-guard?' asks the Leader
of the Chorus: 'Yes, as usual.' 'No. Tell him to
come alone; the body-guard would only frighten
the strangers and make them afraid to speak.'
The Nurse is puzzled, but agrees. Aigisthos returns, suspicious but not suspicious enough. He
enters the house; the Chorus wait as night falls;

there is a shriek, and out rushes a panic-stricken slave exclaiming

> One from the dead doth slay the living!

But to whom can he cry for help? He cries to the strongest human being in the castle precincts, Clytemnestra. She enters; understands in a moment that the avenger is there, and calls for her battle-axe to meet him (891):

> To that, meseemeth, we are come, we two!

Orestes enters before the axe can arrive: 'I was looking for you. I have done with him.' She fights for her life, inch by inch of the way, and states her case in a dialogue of marvellous power and brevity. Orestes nearly yields, but, his purpose confirmed by a word from Pylades, hardens himself and sends her before him into the house. There follows a song of exultation from the Chorus, and then comes the terrific final scene, in which, standing over the dead bodies, Orestes appeals to God, to the Argive people, to the Sun, to attest his innocence, but even while he appeals feels his reason going, and sees the Furies. The Chorus try to comfort him and beg him not to yield to fantasies. There is nothing there! But he answers with the terrible lines (1061 f.)

> You cannot see them, I alone can see.
> I am hunted. I shall never rest again.

There is plot, action, and, of course character,

all through. But the value of every effect depends on the great introductory choruses of the *Agamemnon*, which also lead up to the long final comment at the end of the *Eumenides*, with its deeply felt doctrine of the validity throughout the world of the Law of Justice, and yet the existence in Heaven of a Will or an Understanding that is supreme even over the Law.

For the *Eumenides* also starts, like the *Choëphoroe*, with rapid and almost sensational action. We see the Prophetess of the Temple at Delphi making her formal *Prorrhesis* or prefatory address before entering the Holy Place. She enters, and in a moment returns palsied with terror, having seen at the Altar a man with a bloody sword, and a ring of monstrous beings round him. She creeps away, praying Apollo to purify his own house. The back scene is opened, and we see Orestes at the Altar, Apollo above him, and all around the hideous Furies, in a magic sleep which has been cast upon them. Apollo bids Orestes fly to the Image of Athena at Athens; the sleeping Furies remain. To them enters the Ghost of Clytemnestra, with the open wound in her throat, crying them to wake and not to fail her. As they gradually awaken the Ghost vanishes. They revile Apollo for helping a murderer, and he drives them —'a flock of wild goats unherded'—from his precinct. The scene changes, and we see Orestes worn out with suffering clinging to the image of

Pallas in Athens. He prays, and there is no answer from the goddess. Instead the Avengers arrive, having tracked him by his bleeding feet. They prison him at the Altar. He prays again to Athena, and again there is no answer. The Furies proceed to sing a magical 'binding song', which will make him for ever theirs, unable to escape or move or think. Then, at the very depth of his despair, there enters Athena. After some explanation the Furies, confident of their cause, agree to accept Athena's own decision between them and their guilty victim. Let Orestes be put on his oath; if he can swear that he did not murder his mother, let him go free. To their surprise Athena says that the matter cannot be so decided. There must be a trial and an examination into motives, circumstances, the degree of punishment already suffered, and all else that is relevant. The Furies cannot understand this: it seems an overthrow of the simple Law of Justice—'On him that doeth it shall be done'. The trial takes place; Orestes is acquitted by the casting vote of Athena; and then for about 300 lines, 777–1045, comes the real problem of the drama, which is solved only by the conversion of the Furies into spirits of guardianship and their acceptance of a seat in Athenian soil beside the Areopagus. The vengeance that blindly smites has become the law that protects. Without that long essay in theology—obscure perhaps, but beyond question deeply felt and thought out—the whole drama would have lost its meaning. The tragedy would be a mere melodrama.

The first point, then, which should be emphasized about the *Oresteia* is that in the *Oresteia* for the first time Aeschylus creates the drama of plot and action, as contrasted with the mere impassioned contemplation of a situation which belonged to the original *Molpê* of the tragic chorus; but that, on the other hand, his action is still set in the midst of that contemplation; the issues are deepened and made grander; the deeds and sufferings of individual human creatures are seen, as it were, *sub specie aeternitatis*.[1]

What, then, is the burden of this impassioned contemplation in which all the action of the *Oresteia* is enclosed? It is difficult to state it in modern words without making one of two serious errors; either making each issue too precise and thus transforming contemplation into commonplace dogmatism, or again of misrepresenting Aeschylus' thought by expressing it in the terms of some modern controversy. The second can be avoided by resolutely keeping the issues simple; for the problems which vexed Aeschylus are most of them permanent problems, the same yesterday, to-day, and as far forward as we can see in history; it is only their associations and accretions that have changed with the changes of civilization.

---

[1] See on this point the fine analysis in Prof. Cornford's *Thucydides Mythistoricus*, pp. 144 ff.

The first is, I fear, impossible to avoid, except by a constant effort of imagination.

At the back of all lies the principle of Retribution or Justice: Δράσαντα παθεῖν, 'On him that doeth it shall be done.' This *Dikê*, or law of retribution, has two scopes: it is a law of nature, stating a fact, and also a moral law, enjoining a duty. The sinner both is punished, and ought to be punished. And yet, from the very beginning we have a question: Is that all?

The war against Troy was a punishment of wrong; it was an ἀρωγή, an aid given to the injured. Paris had robbed the House of the Atridae as boys might rob a vulture's nest, and the two parent birds would hover in misery over the empty tree till some pitying spirit—'some Apollo, or Pan or Zeus' (*Ag.* 55)—should avenge their suffering.

Presently we hear of the ὅλιον κράτος, the sign of victory by the way, seen by the army and interpreted by the prophet Calchas. They had seen two eagles tearing a hare with the unborn young in its womb. The prophet knew that the two eagles were the two Kings; the hare was Troy, and the unborn young all her innocent children. We must remember that ancient feeling, more sensitive than modern, regarded with horror this slaying of the unborn. The Sign meant victory, but victory at some appalling price (114–21).

'Twas a king among birds to each of the Kings of the
    Sea,
  One eagle black, one black but of fire-white tail,
By the House, on the spear hand, in station where all
    might see:
And they tore a hare and the life in her womb that grew;
Yea, the life unlived and the races unrun they slew.
  Sorrow, sing sorrow, but good prevail, prevail!

The prophet recognizes the eagles as the two
Kings and reads the omen:

At the last, the last, this Hunt hunteth Ilion down:

.   .   .   .   .   .

If only God's eye gloom not against our gates,
  Till the great War-curb of Troy, fore-smitten, fail.
For Pity lives, and those wingèd hounds she hates
Which tore in the trembler's body the unborn beast;
  Yea, Artemis abhorreth the eagles' feast.
  Sorrow, sing sorrow; but good prevail, prevail.

The vision increases upon him, and he fears this
indignant Pity which abhors the eagles' feast: he
prays to Artemis.

  Yet, Oh fulfil, fulfil The sign of the Eagles' Kill:
  Be the vision accepted, albeit horrible!   (126–45)

Through the riddling of prophetic language the
answer comes quite clearly: the omen means
victory, but victory through sin and cruelty.
Artemis will hate it, but he begs her not to prevent its fulfilment. Let us conquer, even if we
conquer through crime!

  That said, and the omen once definitely accepted, he sees more: if they are to conquer

through crime, a price will be exacted for that crime. He sees the wasting winds of Aulis, the slaying of Agamemnon's own child; and after that, some undescribed vista of further vengeance to come.

Agamemnon knew what was to be the price of victory, and accepted it. Like Napoleon, he might have said: 'One does not make omelettes without breaking eggs!' And I imagine almost all practical conquerors would have agreed with him.

When the fleet was held at Aulis and the prophet demanded the sacrifice of Iphigenia he had one more opportunity of turning back. But the great aim of his life was to take Troy; it was worth some suffering; and, after all, the sacrifice of a royal virgin, hideous as it seemed, was 'Themis'; it was an act known to ancient religious custom. 'I have no right to refuse. May all be well!'

Aeschylus takes great pains to explain the state of mind of a man who yields to this ghastly temptation, and he has to do so, of course, with no scientific psychological language at his command. The whole army was in despair at the delay, and men were beginning to desert.

They cry, they thirst, for a magic to break the spell;
For a Virgin's blood. 'Tis a rite of old, men tell;
And they burn with longing.—O God, may the end
    be well!

To the Thing that Must Be he subdued him slowly,
    And a strange wind within his bosom tossed,
A wind of dark thought, unclean, unholy;
    And he rose up, daring to the uttermost.
For men are boldened by a Blindness, straying
    Toward base desire, which brings grief hereafter,
        Yea, and itself is grief;
So this man hardened to his own child's slaying,
    As help to avenge him for a woman's laughter
        And bring his ships relief.   (214–27)

The same problem of temptation, though in different circumstances, is raised about Paris. His act has brought Troy to destruction; he might have known that it would, but his desire for Helen had made him blind.

The tempting of misery forceth him, the dread
    Child of fore-scheming Woe.
And help is vain; the fell desire within
Is veilèd not, but shineth bright, like Sin:
    And, as false gold will show
Black where the touchstone trieth, so doth fade
His honour in God's ordeal. Like a child,
    Forgetting all, he hath chased his wingèd bird. . .

    Paris to Argos came,
        Love of a woman led him;
So God's altar he brought to shame,
        Robbing the hand that fed him.   (385–402)

So much for the sin of Paris. Then we have a description of the misery of Menelaus when his beloved is gone, a description so wonderful that I dare not quote my inadequate translation, except for the ending. She is gone,

But a shape that is a dream mid the phantoms of the
    night,
Cometh near, full of tears, bringing vain, vain delight;
For in vain when, desiring, he can feel the joy's breath
—Nevermore! Nevermore!—from his arms it vanish-
    eth,
As a bird along the wind-ways of sleep.   (420–26)

One might think that this was the climax; but the
reverse is the case. It is just not the climax.

In the mid castle Hall, on the hearthstone of the
    Kings,
These griefs there be, and griefs passing these.
But in each man's dwelling of the host that sailed the seas
A sad woman waits; she has thoughts of many things,
    And patience in her heart lieth deep.

Faces of them she sent
    Haunt her; but lo, returning
Come in stead of the men that went
    Armour and dust of burning.

And the gold-changer, Ares, who changeth quick for
    dead,
Who poiseth his scale in the striving of the spears,
Back from Troy sendeth dust, heavy dust, wet with
    tears,
Sendeth ashes with men's names in his urns neatly
    spread.
And they weep over the men, and they praise them one
    by one;
How this was a wise fighter, and this nobly slain. . .
    'Fighting to win back another's wife!'
Till a murmur is begun,
    And there steals an angry pain
    Against Kings too forward in the strife.

There by Ilion's gate
  Many a soldier sleepeth,
Young men beautiful; fast in hate
  Troy her conqueror keepeth.

The Elders feel a curse brooding in the air.
It is difficult to see what retribution can overtake
the conquerors now that Troy is destroyed;
nevertheless

My heart waits some tiding that the dark holdeth still,
For of God not unmarked is the shedder of much blood.

And so on to their last prayer:

May I never be a sacker of Cities!   (427–72)

It might be thought from these verses that in this
tremendous sense of the evil of War Aeschylus
was thinking only of the sufferings of his own
people; that the enemy did not matter. But any
such minimizing and belittling of his thought is
impossible in view of certain other passages.

After the beacon message announcing the capture of Troy, Clytemnestra, who is wrought up to
a high pitch of suspense, goes on to describe,
almost as if she saw them, the scenes in the streets
of Troy, the heaps of dead, the wailing women,
the Greeks sick with slaughter and tired out, but
hoping at last for a good night's sleep.

Oh, if these days they keep them free from sin
Toward Ilion's conquered shrines and Them within
Who watch unconquered, maybe not again
The smiter shall be smit, the taker ta'en.

May God but grant there fall not on that host
The greed of gold that maddeneth, and the lust
To spoil inviolate things! The homeward race
Is yet unrun, from goal to starting-place.
Yea, though of God they pass unchallengèd,
Methinks the wrong of those forgotten dead
Might waken, groping for its will! . . . Ye hear
A woman's word, belike a woman's fear.

She apologizes for her somewhat dangerous
language. But why has Aeschylus put in this
remarkable speech? It must be to remind us of
the law that 'On him that doeth it shall be done',
and that 'of God not unmarked is the shedder of
much blood'. In particular it prepares a great
effect in the Herald's speech, when that happy
and, on the whole, kindly person arrives with the
full news of victory. The Herald—by a slight
dramatic licence—comes straight from the battle-
field; he weeps for very thankfulness to be home
again, and to see the faces, divine and human,
that he had left so long. Then he calls for a great
welcome to Agamemnon.

Grand greeting give him! Aye, it need be grand—
Who, God's avenging mattock in his hand,
Hath wrecked Troy's towers and digged her soil
     beneath,
Till her gods' houses, they are things of death,
Her altars waste, and blasted every seed
Whence life might spring! So perfect is his deed,
So dire the yoke on Ilion he hath cast,
The first Atrides, King of Kings at last,
And happy among men!   (524–30)

It is a bad look-out for any one in Greek poetry when he is called 'a happy man'. But here the doom of Agamemnon is made almost certain by the boast of the Herald: he has done exactly the things which, we have been warned, must lead to divine punishment. And more, by accident or design, Aeschylus repeats almost word for word about Agamemnon one of the lines in which Darius in the *Persae* had described the sins which made inevitable the Persians' punishment.

βωμοὶ δ' ἄιστοι καὶ θεῶν ἱδρύματα,
καὶ σπέρμα πάσης ἐξαπόλλυται χθονός.   (*Ag.* 528 f.)

compared with

βωμοὶ δ' ἄιστοι, δαιμόνων θ' ἱδρύματα
πρόρριζα φύρδην ἐξανέστραπται βάθρων. (*Persae,* 811 f.)

The desecration of the Gods' temples, the violation of human sanctities, and—perhaps above all—the awakening of the wound of the dead—ἐγρηγορὸς τὸ πῆμα τῶν ὀλωλότων—make retribution certain. There are many less important passages which might be cited; but the main contention is really quite clear. Agamemnon is himself unconscious of sin; he feels himself rather a favourite of the Gods and a most deserving one. His death on the mere human plane is the result of the blood feud; Aigisthos has the plain duty of avenging his brothers upon their slayer, Atreus, or since Atreus is dead, upon his son Agamemnon. Clytemnestra has also her personal motives: the death of Iphigenîa, Agamemnon's infidelities, and her own

love of Aigisthos. But these mere human motives
are only the instruments of something superhuman and eternal. Clytemnestra herself knows
it. She is not herself; she is only an instrument in
the hand of the Daemon that haunts the house
(1498 ff.).

> And criest thou still this deed hath been
>   My work? Nay, gaze, and have no thought
> That this is Agamemnon's Queen.
>   A Thing not I hath round him wrought
> This phantom of the dead man's wife:
> He, the old Wrath, the Driver of man astray,
>   Pursuer of Atreus for the feast defiled:
> To assoil an ancient debt he hath paid this life.
> A warrior and a crownèd King this day
>   Atones for a torn child.

The murder of the children of Thyestes is taken
as the beginning of all the bloodshed. It was so
easy, so safe, so wicked, to kill those two little
children. Their father fled to die far away in
exile, and ever since then the *Alastor*, the *Driver
Astray*, has possessed the House of Atreus. It is
those children that Cassandra hears sobbing when
she first comes to the house, and afterwards sees
ὀνείρων προσφερεῖς μορφώμασιν, 'like the shapes
in dreams', beating against the walls. But observe
what the *Alastor* does. He drives men mad, no
doubt, but above all he is mad himself. He craves
blood for blood; the blood of vengeance to wash
out the blood of crime; and then more blood
to wash out that (1509 ff.).

On the red Slayer crasheth, groping wild
  For blood, more blood, to find his peace again,
  And wash, like water, the old frozen stain
    Of the torn child.

He seeks his peace by means of more blood; and that is not the way by which Peace is found. Yet is that perhaps the very mistake that all these avengers, all these instruments of *Dikê*, are making?

Turn to the Cassandra scene, the scene selected by the ancient scholiast for his one outburst of admiration. It is very long, and beyond doubt it is tremendously effective as drama: the doomed prophetess, doomed to foresee and foretell and never to be believed, is there at the door, seeing vision after vision which reveal the ancient crimes of the house, the coming murder of Agamemnon, the coming murder of herself. She struggles to warn the Elders, but at first her meaning only comes in the obscure riddles and metaphors of prophecy, and when at last by some violent effort of self-command she contrives to get her statement clear and plain, it is no use. The curse operates, and though the Elders speak kindly to her, they do not believe her. That is, they are all blind; like Agamemnon who must have his army and his victory, like Paris who must have Helen, like the *Alastor* himself who must have the new blood in which to wash the old, they are all working towards their own destruction and, when warned, they do not believe or understand. They

are going the way of the Old Masters of Heaven
who reigned before Zeus: they smite and are
smitten, they are slain and slay the slayer, and
pass away. Ἀράσαντα παθεῖν. Is that the fullness
of *Dikê*? Is there nothing beyond?

Thus we are led to the great problem of the
Eumenides. Clytemnestra has murdered Agamemnon: if the law is to be obeyed Orestes must
avenge his father and slay her. Apollo, the God
of revelation, interpreter of the will of Zeus, has
warned him that he must kill his mother or else
he will lie under dire penalties for the most sacred
of duties unperformed. He slays her; but then
what is to be done to him?

We must realize, of course, from the outset that
Orestes is nowhere accused of ferocity or of yield-
ing to angry passions. In an age before law, the
blood feud took the place of law. The duty of
bringing down the triumphant wrongdoer fell
upon some individual or some small family group.
It was a grievous duty. It meant that the avenger
must live for it alone, in hardship and constant
danger, sacrificing all pleasure in life till he had
saved the honour of the injured dead. We must
realize, too, that to fail in this duty would not in
ancient times be regarded as an act of charity
towards the murderer, but as a lack of pity or
consideration for the murderer's victim. We have
seen in the *Agamemnon* how Pity acts not as a
personal emotion but a sort of world force. Pity

for the injured vultures sent out an Erinys to avenge them; Pity for the hare's young made Artemis demand her heavy price from Agamemnon; Pity for the 'wound of the dead' of Troy made the conqueror a doomed man. In the *Eumenides* the Furies, amid all their ferocity, insist that they are the instruments of Pity. If the mother-murderer is allowed to escape, they argue, strong and brutal man will everywhere be free to violate the old and the weak. There will be no wrath for evil deeds (490–525). When Pallas first asks them who they are, in all their hideousness, they answer that in the houses below the earth, among the injured and helpless dead, they are called Prayers.[1] That is what they are, the prayers of the injured for justice on the oppressor. This is illustrated in the scene with the Ghost of Clytemnestra. It is her suffering, her shame, her starved cry for justice, that inspires the Furies to the pursuit of the murderer. Those who have studied the Apocalyptic literature, and realized the close connexion between the dreams of Hell and the experience of persecution, will appreciate this point of view and get a glimpse of the chain of thought which made Dante attribute the creation of Hell to *La somma Sapienza e il primo Amore*. Hell is the prayer of the persecuted for some world which will do justice on the wicked.

[1] Ἀραί *Eum.* 417. They are prayers for vengeance rather than what we call 'curses'.

Blood cries for blood; the injured man cries for justice: the prayer of the forgotten dead lives and works. That is *Dikê*, the inevitable law. And the Furies, being the personification of that Prayer and that cry, are not cold Judges distributing well-weighed dooms, they are an incarnate passion for avenging the sufferer and smiting the wicked. Several of the choruses in the *Eumenides*, like several in the *Bacchae*, seem to be divided between a band of raging Maenads and a band of musing philosophers. The philosophers explain the theory of punishment and its necessity; the Maenads leap and shout after their prey, they smell the trail of blood, they exult in the victim's torment. In a very interesting passage Apollo expels them from his temple as being un-Hellenic: they belong to the stage of civilization which gouges eyes and lops off heads and castrates and mutilates and impales by due sentence of law, so that the land is filled with the agonized moaning of tortured men (*Eum.* 186 ff.). He is thinking of Persia and Asia generally. We may think of the Law Courts of the Middle Ages and the hideous arsenal of implements of torture which characterized, for example, French and German law up to the time of Voltaire. When indignation against wickedness becomes a passion we all know what a wicked passion it can be. The Furies themselves are never satiated: they hunt their victim to death, and he is not free even when dead. It is not in them to forgive; if they forgave, they would cease to be themselves: for they only exist as instruments of the Law, Δράσαντα παθεῖν, παθεῖν τὸν ἔρξαντα, *On him that doeth it shall be done.* All the rage of the Furies, the long-nursed hate of Clytemnestra, the Pity of Artemis, are all instruments of the Law. It matters little if there is no human avenger living. There is none for Troy; Aeschylus' Cassandra never thinks of herself as such. But the ocean of blood and tears in that dead city swells the whole volume of wrath or pity that is seeking Agamemnon's death. Well may Clytemnestra cry from her heart: 'It is not I that have slain Agamemnon.' Well may Orestes in his turn say to her: 'It is not I that will kill thee; it is thyself': σύ τοι σεαυτήν, οὐκ ἐγώ, κατακτενεῖς (*Cho.* 923). Not Aigisthos, not Clytemnestra, not Orestes; but the Law, however we phrase it, by whatever instrument it works, is the true and inevitable slayer. The Law works.

That being so, how can there be any forgiveness? 'All things pay atonement to one another for their injustice according to the rule of time.'[1] If that is the Law, how can any one escape? Are we not tied down to a wheel of revolving retribution, unending, mechanical, and ultimately, if we think it out, futile?

As we noticed above, and as I have tried to explain elsewhere, Aeschylus had already hinted

[1] Anaximander, fr. 9 Diels.

at his answer: 'If I seek to cast off from my mind
τὸ μάταν ἄχθος, the burden of futility, though I
sink my plummet through the universe, I can find
nothing to help me but Zeus . . . Zeus, who made
for man a road to Thought, who established as an
abiding law the power of Learning by Suffering'
(*Ag.* 163–83). That is the Zeus who delivers us
from the burden of futility, from the never-
ending chain of vengeances reavenged. It is the
same Zeus who, in the *Supplices*, brought peace
and bliss to the wandering Io, and through her
brought into existence the Saviour of mankind,
Heracles: the same Zeus who, in the later part
of the Prometheus trilogy, forgave his enemies
the Titans and set Prometheus free. True, he is
one of those βιαίως σέλμα σεμνὸν ἡμένων 'by strife
lifted to the throne of the world'; he was fierce in
his first years of rule (*Ag.* 180; *Pr.* 35). But,
unlike all who were before him, he can think and
learn and forgive. We are told in the *Eumenides*
that he instituted the Law of the Suppliant: the
man who throws away all defence and puts himself at your mercy must be respected. The first
suppliant was the blood-stained Ixion, and Zeus
pardoned and cleansed him. To betray or reject
a suppliant is, in the eyes of Zeus, the worst of
sins, 'unforgivable even in the grave' (*Suppl.* 416).
Nay, there is a further extension of the same
sentiment. In some mystical sense, just as Zeus
the protector of Kings is himself a King, as

Hermes the god of heralds is himself a Herald,
as he to whom the bull is sacrificed is himself a
Bull, so Zeus the Protector of Suppliants is himself
a Suppliant, Zeus Aphictor (*Suppl.* 1). That
power which listens to the cry of the robbed
vulture and the young of the slaughtered hare,
which feels the wound of the Trojan dead, that
'Apollo or Pan or Zeus' whose indignant pity
demands judgement on the offender, demands
also, at its own good time, his forgiveness. I have
tried to show elsewhere how the Trial in the
Eumenides is decided by one consideration only:
the will of Zeus. Apollo is simply the προφήτης
Διός, the interpreter of Zeus; he has never uttered
from his throne of prophecy any word which was
not commanded by Zeus: therefore Zeus himself
ordered Orestes to avenge his father.[1] Athena is
the daughter of Zeus, created by him alone, with
no mother. She is 'completely the Father's', pure
undiluted Zeus (738, 826). And she acquits the
prisoner.

This conception of a God who is above the Law
and can therefore forgive is the great contribution
made to the religion of Europe by Greek anthropomorphism. With all its innumerable faults,
anthropomorphism had this merit, as compared
with either the fetishism of various savage religions, pre-Hellenic and modern, or the noble
impersonality of Buddhism. Plutarch insists that

[1] *Eum.* 19, 616 ff.

the world 'is not governed by fabulous Typhons and Giants, but by One who is a wise Father to all' (*Vit. Pelop.* xxi). Plato argues that the rule of 'a man of wise and royal nature' is vastly superior to a mere rule of law, because the law cannot cover all the infinite diversities of human life and, when it happens not to fit, cannot think out what is right but 'like some very stubborn and ignorant man' goes on insisting that its exact orders must be carried out (*Politicus,* 294*a*). Similarly Aristotle in discussing *Epieikeia,* or the higher Equity, expects the Law to be 'corrected' by 'a wise or sensible man'. Aeschylus only develops, with the imagination of a poet, an idea which lies at the heart of the anthropomorphic conception of God.[1]

Thus the first problem of the *Eumenides,* viz. the question why Orestes is acquitted and how any such reversal of the Law of *Dikê* is possible, can, I think, be solved along lines which are consonant with ancient thought as a whole and quite characteristic of the thought of Aeschylus. The second problem is the conversion of the Furies from hellish spirits of torment, lusting for blood and pain, into beneficent spirits, protecting Athens, averting civil strife, giving peace to the household and fruitfulness to the soil and the flocks; their conversion, in fact, from Erinyes to Eumenides. I get some light on this question

[1] Cf. *Five Stages of Greek Religion,* pp. 80 ff.

from a remark of Mr. Claude Montefiore about
St. Paul. St. Paul's language about the Law, he
says, shows that he was not a real Jew brought up
in a Jewish atmosphere. He looks on the Law as
an alien and almost hostile thing; a set of arbitrary
rules for breaking which a man is condemned
and punished and conscience-haunted. A true Jew
looks upon the Law as an ideal of pure and good
life, easy to follow, and bringing Man into connexion with God. The parallel is, of course, not
exact; but it is helpful. The Erinyes are the Law
of Justice seen from the outside by those on whom
it is imposed, Law as the terror of the transgressor.
The Eumenides are the Law seen from the inside
by those to whom it is not alien but a thing of
their own, an ideal to keep human society at
peace with itself and with God. And what exactly is the change that has taken place in the
Furies, to explain this change of attitude in the
play? It is that they have given up their claim
for a purely mechanical working of the Law that
the Doer must Suffer, and have accepted Athena's
principle that not only the deed shall be considered but everything that caused or surrounded
the deed. They accept πειθοῦς σέβας, the sanctity
of the spirit which persuades and hears Persuasion;
that is, they will listen to Persuasion and will think
again. They become no longer a mechanical
Law of Retribution which operates blindly; but
a Law which thinks and feels and seeks real

Justice. In such a conception, as we are told in the last words of the trilogy, Zeus who sees all and Moira, or the blind Law of what must be, are united: Ζεὺς ὁ πανόπτας οὕτω Μοῖρά τε συγκατέβα.

How little we know! Or rather, considering the vast interval of time and change and circumstance which lies between us and the Athenians of the fifth century B.C., how astonishing it is that we can get into contact with them at all! The fact is there. Our pronunciation of Greek is all wrong, we know almost nothing effective about their music or dancing, it needs a great imaginative effort to reach even the most tentative comprehension of the background of their thought; yet we do understand something, we do feel. Aeschylus puts together a few words in a particular rhythm; we understand his meaning; we feel the exquisite beauty of that particular collocation of words, and our hearts leap with the loveliness of the rhythm. I have often marvelled how it is that, in Greek poetry, the use of some Doric or Aeolic form gives a charm which an average modern scholar can quite distinctly appreciate. How can such an infinitely frail thing live so long and so vividly?

If my understanding of this poet whom I have loved and studied since I was an undergraduate is approximately right, it would seem that there are three things, among others, for which he is greatly memorable.

He began the technique of stage-land: he
reached this way and that, made daring experiments, overthrew them and made others, and
eventually led towards a great simplicity and
severity of technique which owed much to the
poet and little to the stage-carpenter.

Secondly, through him ἡ τραγῳδία ἀπεσεμνύνθη:
taking his subjects from the great mass of myth
and fable, often trivial enough, that lay before
his generation, he raised everything he touched
to grandeur. The characters in his hands became
heroic; the conflicts became tense and fraught
with eternal issues.

Thirdly, he possessed to a marked degree a
characteristic often found in ancient Greek poets;
he was a thinker, and an impassioned thinker, as
well as a teller of tales and writer of verses. I
have tried to indicate, so far as the seven extant
plays provide evidence, the lines of thought which
seem most definitely characteristic of Aeschylus.
His earliest play begins with 'Zeus the Suppliant',
his last ends with a Zeus who understands and can
forgive, thereby fulfilling, not annulling, the true
Law of Justice. Aeschylus was a soldier in a great
and famous war. He took part in a terrible disaster
and in one of the world's most celebrated victories.
His descriptions of war in the *Agamemnon* and the
Seven against Thebes show that he knew what it
was like, and almost his last words about it are the
prayer: 'May I never be a conqueror.' Stress is

sometimes laid upon the close approach to monotheism which is found in Aeschylus' conception of Zeus; but the Greeks paid comparatively little attention to the problem whether, as they would put it, 'the divine is one or many'. I should lay more stress on his conception of a Divine Power which thinks, understands, and learns by suffering, and of a Divine Pity which broods over all the Hubris and cruelty of the world: over the robbed bird and the hunted hare, the suppliant Danaids, the crucified Prometheus, the besieged Theban women, and the innumerable dead in Troy, as well as over the murdered Clytemnestra and the haunted Orestes. Do not let us say that such thoughts are 'modern'. The mourning woman that waited in every house of the men that sailed for Troy had in some ways exactly the same thoughts as the mourning woman who waited in other houses during the years 1914 to 1918. Such thoughts and the reflections about them are neither modern nor ancient. They live with mankind always.

CHAPTER VII

APPENDIX: A SCENARIO OF THE AGAMEMNON

THIS appendix raises and tries to answer a number of questions which often escape the notice both of editors of the text and of commentators. The term 'Scenario' is not quite exact. It is a common practice in theatres, before a play is put into rehearsal, to call the company together, and let the author give a preliminary reading, much abbreviated, with comments, so that the various actors may have some notion of what they are expected to feel and do. It is something like that which is the purpose of the present notes, except that a mere commentator's conjectures have to take the place of the dramatist's own authoritative directions.

The Trilogy

The whole trilogy hangs together: it is a drama with one theme: How is the law of Justice (*Dikê*) to admit the possibility of forgiveness? The law is mechanical, automatic, unfailing: the final answer is that above the Law is a Father or King who can understand and therefore pardon.

Thus in the *Agamemnon* we have *Avenging Justice*. Successful and triumphant wrongdoing by the strong against the helpless at last becomes

intolerable. The wealth and power of the House
of Atreus are no defence against the law of *Dikê*
or the indignant pity of the Gods (135 ff.). To
pay for the sins in the sack of Troy, the slaying of
Iphigenîa and—worst of all—the old brutal crime
of his father against the children of Thyestes,
Agamemnon must die. When that atonement is
made, is that the end? Clytemnestra hopes so
(1576 f., 1673), but we know that it cannot be.
In the *Choëphoroe* the slayers of Agamemnon,
whatever their claims, must die. Orestes, the only
son of the murderęd man, is bound to avenge him,
even though this involves killing his mother, the
most horrible, on the face of it, of all crimes.
Apollo, the mouthpiece of Zeus, demands it.

In the third play the furies, representing the
mechanical law of Dikê or Moira, demand that
the slayer of these slayers must also die. But is
this chain of senseless vengeances to go on for
ever? No. Orestes slew by the will of Zeus,
expressed by Apollo (616 f.) and Zeus, through
the mouth of Athena (797 f.; cf. 763, 663 ff.),
acquits him. Ζεὺς ὁ πανόπτας οὕτω Μοῖρά τε συγκατέβα. Zeus the All-seeing and Moira come
together and the Avenging Spirits accept the rule
of Law.

The Agamemnon

Scene I. Night. Castle of Atridae. Watchman on
roof, sleepy, watching.

Very quiet opening. At the words ὀρφναίου

πυρός FLASH of beacons. Watchman shouts for
Queen to rise, sacrifice (58), and start an OLOLUG-
MOS or Women's Triumph Cry over the sacrifice.
Of course she does so and the repeated Ololugmos
is an important feature in the play. (Cf. 587
ἀνωλόλυξα μέν, 595–7 ὀλολυγμὸν ἄλλος ἄλλοθεν
κατὰ πτόλιν, 1236 ἐπωλολύξατο . . . ὥσπερ ἐν
μάχης τροπῇ: cf. 475–87 πόλιν Διήικι θοὰ βάξις.)
Exit WATCHMAN.

Enter CLYTEMNESTRA with a crowd of Propoloi.
Stir and noise. They make Ololugmos, kindle
the altars, then *exeunt* to spread the Triumph
Cry (595).

Clytemnestra stays alone (84 ff.) like Aeschylus' other silent figures (Ar. *Frogs.* 911 ff.), in an
agony of silent prayer at an altar (cf. 973). She
has been safe while he was away. Now he is
returning; it will be his death or hers.

Enter the ELDERS. They have not heard the
Ololugmos and know nothing of the beacon till
they see Clytemnestra and notice the flames upon
all the altars (83–96). They ask her to speak, but
she rises silently and goes out, probably at 103.
(They refer to her silence later, 263.)

Parodos

'The tenth year of the war; the war was an
'Αρωγή, a help to the injured, a righting of wrong,
i.e. redress for the wrong done to Menelaus. All
wrong leads to Δίκη. If even a vulture's nest is

robbed, there is One above, "*some Pan or Zeus or Apollo*", who pities and exacts retribution. Hence long suffering of Greek and Trojan alike; and who knows the end? We were too old to go to the war; we are now weak shadows, dreams lost in daylight.'

Why this emphasis on their weakness? It is preparation for 1343. At the critical moment Agamemnon must be alone and helpless. Menelaus is away (618–80, cf. *Od.* γ. 249, also *Ag.* 257 μονόφρουρον, 1103 f. ἀλκὰ 2' ἑκὰς ἀποστατεῖ). More than once Agamemnon is on the verge of being warned: cf. the language of the Leader to the Herald (539–50, 615 f.), to Agamemnon himself (788 ff.), and of course the Cassandra scene.

104 ff., 'We can tell the story: two eagles were seen tearing a hare with young: Αἴλινον, αἴλινον εἰπέ. That is ἀνόσιον, unholy!' Calchas explained: the eagles are the Atridae, Troy the hare (144); *the omen means Victory plus Crime plus the wrath of Artemis!* Will Agamemnon accept it? 'Yes; with all its consequences.' Thereupon Calchas sees (146–55) a vista of them: Iphigenîa's death, Clytemnestra's vengeance . . . more beyond. 'Apollo the Healer, help us!'

160 ff. 'Is it for ever thus, punishment on punishment unescapeable? No; there is always Zeus, who gives the power to *learn by suffering, to think, get wisdom.*' It is significant that this kind of trochaic stanza does not recur till *Eum.* 916, in the songs of reconciliation.

'I turn aside from these lower gods to Zeus, whate'er He be: only in Him can I get away from this burden of endless, senseless, revenges. He shows man the way to learn, to think, till against his will he can learn *Sophrosynê* (Wisdom, or Mercy).'

Story of the sacrifice of Iphigenîa, and a study of the temptation by which Agamemnon was led into such madness.

'Her cry (237) will be a curse on his house for ever. The craft of Calchas had its way. What can the end be? Only may the future be better than the past. So prays this *sole guard* of the land.'

Enter CLYTEMNESTRA *in state.*

She has prayed (cf. 973 f.) and thought, and is ready. This news means for her either death or triumph, her death or his. She accepts the battle with joy. 264 εὐάγγελος μέν: cf. 895–902, τἀναγκαῖον ἐκφυγεῖν ἅπαν. 1377 ff. ἀγὼν ὅδ' οὐκ ἀφρόντιστος.

264 ff. 'Good news! Troy is taken.'—'Impossible!'—'Yet true.'—'How do you know? When did it fall?' BEACON SPEECH.

Inorganic? Greek tragedy liked brilliant speeches of description, (cf. the storm 636 ff., the war 551 ff.) even when not made necessary by the drama. (Strongest instance, the chariot race in Soph. *El.* 680–763.) Here justified by the need of some explanation of Clytemnestra's knowledge; also probably by contemporary interest in the strange system of telegraphy, said to be Persian. Cf. the geographical speeches in *Prom.* and *Suppl.*

LEADER, thrilled by the wonderful speech, says 'Go on' (320 ff.).

SPEECH on the Ἰλίου Πέρσις, highly important for drama and character. (The Sack of Troy was a traditional theme of horror, cf. the Cyclic *Iliu Persis* and *Little Iliad*, and the *Troades*.) (1) Misery of Trojans, men, women, and children. The Greeks can at last sleep at night—and plunder all day. (2) 'I only pray they may avoid offences against holy things—against the gods of Troy and the gods' temples. If not . . . it is still a long way to reach home and safety.' 'And even if there is no offence (ἀναμπλάκητος) (or, reading ἐναμπλάκητος, if there is offence) against the gods, the wound of the dead may become wakeful, seeking for some sudden stroke. . . . Forgive a woman's fears!'

Obviously her fears are largely her disguised wishes. If only Agamemnon could be destroyed before reaching home! Hence she fears she has said too much, and apologizes. She is only a woman! A similar note is struck in 1661 (ὧδ' ἔχει λόγος γυναικός) where her woman's heart craves for peace. *Exit* CLYTEMNESTRA.

Stasimon, 367–474

The destruction of Troy is the punishment of Sin. It is always so. Why then do men sin, knowing what the end must be? The process of temptation described: man pursues his desire 'like a winged bird', forgetting all else (cf. Agamemnon's temptations, 218 ff.). Paris's sin:

Helen's departure: despair of Menelaus. Grief for
him, but worse grief for the people of all Hellas.
A weeping woman in every house:[1] the return of
the ashes: the dead who shall never return. The
growing pain and anger everywhere against the
Atridae, so forward in the fight. *The shedder of
much blood does not escape the eye of God* (461).
May I never be a sacker of cities, nor yet a
conquered prisoner!' (472)—Evidently God will
exact Δίκη for the Sack of Troy.

475–87 Conversation among the Elders. They
hear the Ololugmos. 'A noise of voices running
through the city. True?'—'No; woman's talk.'
—'Just like a woman's sceptre (i.e. her method of
government), she believes what she hopes.'—'The
rumour of women's voices quickly comes to
nothing.'

487. μετανάστασις χοροῦ. So talking *Exeunt* the
Elders (*vide* Blomfield's Edition (1826), p. 13)
or make some evolution equivalent to a fall of the
curtain. Presently they return. Some days have
passed. (This answers Verrall.)

LEADER. Now we shall soon know. I see a
Herald, still covered with the dried dust which is
the neighbour and sister of the mud of battle.
He will tell us all.

The Herald is pictured as coming straight from
the battle: cf. Orestes' new-drawn sword and
bloody hands in *Eum.* 41 f.

[1] I take πένθεια to be a feminine of πενθεύς, 'a mourner'.

Enter HERALD. He runs in and kisses the ground, weeping for joy. *Purpose of scene twofold.* (1) His impulsive loving delight at seeing his home again forms a strong contrast to the cold hard pride of Agamemnon, 810 ff. (2) His proud description of the horrors and crimes committed in Troy (like those which brought the wrath of God on the Persians, *Pers.* 810), coming after Clytemnestra's warning, show Hubris crying to Heaven for punishment.

503–680. 'Beloved land, at last, after ten years! Beloved sunlight; and ye gods of Argos! Prepare to welcome Agamemnon, who brings light to God and man. He has utterly uprooted Troy with the mattock of avenging Zeus. *Her altars are broken to fragments, and the shrines of her gods; and every seed from which the land might rise again is utterly destroyed.* There is a victory for you! And there at last is a *Happy Man!*' (We listen to his boasts in horror; if that is how Agamemnon has acted, doom is certain.)

538–50. Brief dialogue, serving to show trouble at home. Enough to disturb, not enough to provide security. Had they been a little more explicit, Agamemnon would have been saved. (πάλαι τὸ σιγᾶν, cf. 788 ff.)

551–82. WAR SPEECH. Splendid realism of detail: the hard quarters, failure of rations, vermin, cold and heat; but no special dramatic service, except perhaps to suggest the false hope that already τὸ εὖ νενίκηκεν.

585. *Enter* CLYTEMNESTRA. She mentions the

Ololugmos throughout the city and the sacrificial
fires. Dramatically, the speech is her defiant welcome. 'I was right about the beacons. Now bid
him come to the city that longs for him, and *may
he find a wife to suit his heart!*' *Exit* 612.

(613–16 I do not understand. Possibly two
speakers: 613 f. admiring her speech; 615 f. ob-
scurely warning the Herald.)

618–80. The absence of Menelaus: the STORM
SPEECH. Simply a development of *Od.* γ. 249 ff. τοῦ
Μενέλαος ἔην; Menelaus' disastrous absence was
part of the traditional story.

681–745. The HELEN CHORUS. Necessary for the
tradition. But also relevant to the theme: Helen
sweet at first, bitter in the end, like Sin above,
385–95, like the lion's whelp, 717–36. It is Sin,
not mere prosperity, that brings retribution. Hubris
breeds Hubris; Dikê decides the end, the power of
wealth falsely glorified is as naught against her.
(Cue.)

Enter AGAMEMNON's Pompê, typifying 'Wealth
falsely glorified'. A long magnificent entrance
procession, lasting through the anapaests, 783–809.
CASSANDRA is in a chariot behind Agamemnon's,
but is not yet conspicuous.

783–809. CHORUS. 'Hail, Conqueror, Sacker
of Cities!' (Note the ill-omened word). 'Let us
be neither churlish nor servile. We know there
are such things as false flatterers. There are some
now pretending to rejoice, but really not rejoicing.
However, the good shepherd knows his sheep, and
you will detect them. As for us, we are frank. We
were against the war—war to recover a wanton

woman!—but now "All is well that ends well".
You will soon know the true and the false among
your citizens.'

A warning again, but too indefinite to save him.
The procession has stopped. AGAMEMNON speaks
from the chariot. The speech is hard, cold, proud.
No word of humility before God, or love of country,
or affection for any one.

810–54. 'I must first greet the gods who
helped me in the vengeance I took on Troy. A
whole city for one woman! Their glory is now
ashes, and my lion has drunk his fill of the blood
of kings. As for your words of warning, I agree
with all you say. All men are envious; friendship
a pretence and a shadow. No one at Troy was
true to me—except Odysseus, who was taken
against his will! For the rest, I mean to hold
councils, and then, while preserving what is
healthy, *to cut and burn what needs medicine.*
Now I will go in and greet the gods who guided
me to Troy and have brought me safe home.'

The speech has damned Agamemnon but also
alarmed Clytemnestra; how much does he know?
Why is he so suspicious, so utterly unfriendly?
Meantime she must speak her greeting here in
public before the Elders, who certainly know her
guilt, to him, who perhaps knows it. She must find
out; at the worst she can make some attempt to
explain herself before she dies. In places she is
reckless, in places near to hysteria (866–73), but
she carries through.

855. CLYT. 'Elders of Argos, you know I am the sort of woman who cannot live without her man. I am not ashamed, now, after so long, to admit it. I pined all the time he was away. It is a monstrous thing for a woman to be left alone with no man near, in a great house, surrounded by spiteful tongues; and rumours always coming, one upon another, full of evil to the house! Had he been wounded as often as they said, he must be as full of holes as a net; had he been killed as often, he must be some monster like Gêryon with many lives. . . . No wonder I tried to hang myself!'

877. She addresses the King himself.

'You are surprised not to find our child Orestes here? Our war-friend Strophios invited me to send him to Phocis; Argos was not safe, when you were away. I am sure he was sincere in his offer.'

So far Agamemnon has not shown any sign of suspicion. She feels safer.

'As for me, by now my eyes are dry. I have no tears left, always thinking of you, waiting for the beacon. And in dreams I saw you, all girt with terrors—too many for the time I slept. But now, it is all over: this day is port after long seas, dawn after stormy night, water to the parched traveller. May the gods not envy us now! We have suffered enough in the past. Now, beloved face, descend; but never set on bare earth thy foot, O King, the foot that trampled Troy! Handmaids, lay down the tapestries; let all his path be red, and Justice guide him to a home that he never hoped for!'

This wonderful speech is greatly compressed. A more advanced technique would, no doubt, have developed the changes of emotion at greater length and more clearly. Agamemnon receives it coldly, and his feelings remain hidden.

914–57. AGAMEMNON. 'A speech worthy of the occasion, but the compliments would have come better from a third person.—As for the tapestries, do not treat me like a woman, or a barbarian. Tapestries are for the gods.—I should really be afraid to walk on them.—I mean, honour me only as a man should be honoured.— Foot-mats and those tapestries, you know, are different things.—And the greatest gift of God is not to make some fatal mistake (μὴ κακῶς φρονεῖν).'

Observe his nervously repeated objections; the repetition shows his irresolution.

The incident of the crimson tapestries is curious. See note at end, p. 254 Clytemnestra's motive is a wish to make him offend both the gods and the people by his pride: his motive is that pride itself. He would not have walked on the tapestries if left to himself, but secretly he longs to do so.

930–43. Dialogue. CLYT.: 'After all, Priam would have done it. As for envy, how can a great man avoid it?'—AG. 'You really want me to?'

944–56. 'Well, if you insist. My boots must be taken off, and I pray that the jealousy of god be not awakened.'

Movement; descent from chariot, &c., which perhaps first makes CASSANDRA conspicuous.

'This Trojan woman must be treated kindly. God loves a merciful conqueror.' (*Ironic effect.*) 'And she was my special prize of honour from the army.—So, since you compel me, I enter my house treading sea-crimson dyes.'

CLYT. 'There is plenty of purple in the sea; your House has riches abundant. And I would have vowed more than this to have you safe home.—Now all grief is gone; the hour has come. The true Master is in his house.'

Exit AGAMEMNON into House. *Ololugmos* from CLYTEMNESTRA and all the handmaids, which CASSANDRA hears (1236).

—'O Zeus, fulfil my prayers. Do not forget!' Clytemnestra follows him into the house.

The intended victim is now in the house of the murderer; there follows a low, boding chorus, such as is usually followed in Greek tragedy by the death-cry of the victim.

975. CHOR. 'Why am I frightened? The army is home again, the war over. Yet still I am afraid. . . . All is so safe, so prosperous. Yet that is the dangerous state. Everything can be cured except death. Death never. After all no one chain of causes works alone; others cut across it, and one may cancel another; else my inward anguish would break through all barriers and shriek aloud.'

The great door opens: is it Death? No. It is Clytemnestra. What can she want?

1035. CLYT. '*I want you too.* (To Cassandra, who stands terrified and silent.) You have nothing to fret about (ἀμηνίτως). You will be a slave like the rest. We treat our slaves properly, neither better nor worse than they ought to be treated.'

Pause. Cassandra silent, trembling. Leader of Chorus intervenes.

L. 'It is you she means. Captive as you are, you had better go with her, though we understand your feeling.'

Clytemnestra is mortally anxious. She cannot leave this *clairvoyante* outside to warn the Elders, yet if she does not return some one inside may warn Agamemnon.

CLYT. 'She is not a Greekless barbarian; I am using words she can understand, and still trying persuasion.'

L. 'Go with her. It is best. Come down from the chariot.'

CLYT. 'I cannot wait out here. If you mean to obey me, be quick. If words are lost on you,' turning to the Chorus Leader, '*you* show her with dumb hand' [or possibly 'with a hand that talks her language.'].

L. (making signs to Cassandra) 'She certainly does need an interpreter. She is trembling like a wild beast newly caught.'

CLYT. 'She is mad, and giving way to her folly. She will need a curb that makes her mouth

bleed before she understands she is a prisoner.—
I will not stay to be insulted!'

Exit into the Palace.

L. 'I am only sorry for her. Come, poor
woman, leave the chariot, and take up your yoke.'

Does Cassandra leave the chariot now or at 1177?
Either possible. It may be that she has hardly the
self-mastery for so large an action yet, and can only
wait cowering.

1072–1330. CASSANDRA SCENE.

Observe two movements: (1) Cassandra struggling towards clearness. (2) The curse of disbelief
working on the Elders, without their knowledge. At
first they do not understand; when forced to understand they do not believe, and quickly forget. Cf. 1213
ἡμῖν γε μὲν δὴ πιστά, 1246 Ἀγαμέμνονός σέ φημι.

As to Cassandra's struggle, normally a prophetess
like the Pythia is in a state of possession, crying out
in inarticulate or half-articulate paroxysms. Only by
a conscious and painful effort (1214 f., cf. 1182) can
she dominate the paroxysm so as to speak clearly.
(For the Pythia the priests acted as interpreters.)

In the lyric scene, 1070–1176, there is a progress
in clearness, detail being added to detail up to
1139; then a more general lament. Thus:

1072. (1) CA. *'Apollo my destroyer!'* L. 'The
bright Apollo? He does not like people who weep.'

1086. CA. 'Where have you brought me?' L. 'To
the Atridae's House.' 1090 CA. (2) 'No: *a place
for killing men:* a blood-splashing floor.' L. 'She
is right in that; she can find bloodshed here.'

1095. (3) CA. 'A sound of crying; close by: little *children, murdered* for their father to eat. . . .'
L. 'We know of your fame as a prophet. But we do not want any prophets now.'

1100. (4) CA. *'Another awful deed coming*: what is it? It is in the house; and no help near!' L. 'I don't understand this.—Of course every one knows about the children.'

1107. (5) CA. *'A woman* . . . on her husband! Washing him . . . a hand reaching out. . . .'
L. 'I can't make it out. First riddles, and then purblind oracles!'

1114. (6) CA. 'Ah, now it is showing . . . *a net* of death? No, the woman is the net, *she shares the murder.*—Now Erinyes, lift up your voices!'
L. 'What Erinys does she call? My heart stands still with fear: misfortune comes so quick.'

1125. (7) CA. 'Ah, keep the wild bull from his mate! *Tangled in the robe* . . . she smites: he falls in the vessel of water.' (With an effort to be clear) *'I am telling you what is happening in the murderous bath!'*
L. 'I do not claim to be an interpreter of prophecies. And what use have they ever been?'

1136 f. (8) CA. 'Oh, who is that poor woman? What a miserable thing!—It is my death, thrown in with the other.' (Coming half out of the trance, with a shriek) 'Where have you brought me? Just to share your death? What else?'

1146. L. 'You are borne on the breath of God, singing your sorrows like the nightingale.'

CA. 'Ah, the sweet nightingale! Her end was peaceful. I shall be torn by the spear.'

L. 'Whence comes this ghastly music of evil? Whence its guidance?'

1156. CA. 'Alas for the wooing of Paris! Alas for the banks of Scamander where I played! I shall soon be on the banks of Cocytus and Acheron.'

1162. L. '*Ah, that at last is clear, too clear.* It stabs me to the heart, it shatters me.' (For a moment they seem to overcome the curse, but only for a moment.)

1167. CA. 'Oh, the labours of the city, the dead city; the sacrifices of my father before the walls! All in vain! The city is gone, and I shall soon be in the dust, struggling.' (βαλῶ as in *Od.* λ. 424.)

L. 'These words are like the last. Some malignant spirit is upon you making you utter these ghastly oracles. *But what it means I cannot guess.*'

Cassandra with a great effort at self-control ceases her song, and speaks. She has a definite plan. If she first shows that she can read the past, they will believe her when she reads the future.

1178. CA. I will make it clear however it hurts me. Follow me closely.—This House ... there is a band of singers about it, drunk with blood, sister Furies. The beginning of evil, they tell, was a brother's bed merciless to its defiler. Am I right? *Swear to me that I know the past.*'

L. 'What good is an oath? But certainly I am amazed. You know the ancient secrets of this house as if you had stood by and seen the things done.'

1202–13. Explanation of her gift of seer-craft and the curse that accompanied it. She had been through the ritual practice that followed betrothal, but then denied Apollo more. The Leader assures her, '*We at any rate believe you*' (1213 ἡμῖν γε μὲν Δὴ πιστά) and she would have gone on to explain the danger to Agamemnon, when a paroxysm falls upon her.

1214. CA. (Speech 2). 'Oh agony!—Bloody children haunting the house! Vengeance for them. The craven lion against the noble lion. The husband-murderess, the hellish monster with her *Ololugmos* of triumph at his return! (1236). . . . No one believes me. What does it matter? . . . It will come.'

1242. L. 'I understood about Thyestes' children, but then I lost the thread.'

CA. (At last getting the truth clearly said) '*I tell you, you shall look on Agamemnon's death.*'

L. 'Peace, unhappy one! Do not say such things!'

CA. 'No god of peace is here.'

L. 'Not if it were true! But God forbid that it should be.

CA. 'You pray; they kill.'

L. 'What man could do it?'

CA. 'Man! You have indeed missed everything!'

L. 'I do not see any plan by which it could be done.'

CA. 'Yet I speak Greek.'

L. 'So does the Delphic oracle, but it is hard to understand all the same.'

> Another paroxysm. She sees a ball of fire or light. It comes at her— a common experience in modern trances.

1256. CA. (Speech 3) 'Oh, the fire! It is coming at me! Oh, agony. The lioness, coupled with the wolf, will kill me too.'

> Puts her hand to her brow and feels the Stemmata.

'Why keep these mockeries?' (Tears them off and tramples on them; then comes to and sees what she has done in her trance.) 'See, Apollo himself stripping me of his emblems! He brings me first to public scorn, and now to death. A block of death for me, as an altar of death for my father. But an Avenger comes, mother-slayer, father-avenger! The gods have sworn it.—Why should I care, now that Troy has fallen? Why should I mind when her conquerors perish too?— I will go to my death. Only may it be swift.'

> Begins movement towards Palace.

1295–1312. L. 'If it is death, why go to meet it?'

CA. 'There is no escape.' (Goes towards door, and starts back) 'Faugh!'

L. 'Why that disgust?'

CA. 'A smell of blood!'

L. 'Yes, the sacrificed animals.'

CA. 'A vapour, as from a charnel house!'

L. 'That is only the smoke of the incense.'

Doubtless L. is right: the real smell and smoke are *points de repère*. Cf. *Cho.* 1047, where the mention of ϑράκοντες leads to Orestes seeing them.

1313. CA. (Speech 4) 'I will go.—May death be all they want of me.—Strangers, on the day when a woman dies for me, and a man for this ill-wedded man, then bear me witness that I spoke the truth.' (L. 'Oh, we pity you.') 'I would say one word more—one lament over my death. I pray to this last sunlight that I shall ever see, that the Avengers may remember the woman-slave as well as the King. Alas for the life of man! Its prosperity is only a picture, and misfortune like a wet sponge will blot it out.'

Exit into the Palace.

1331. CHOR. 'Great fortune is dangerous. Is death now threatening this victorious King?'

A low, boding chorus, like 1035 ff., but here really followed by the death-cry of Agamemnon within. It is a question for the dramatist how to use the Chorus of Elders. We are prepared for their being helpless (82, 257), which indeed is necessary for the story. Aeschylus follows a plan that is both natural and effective. The men naturally hesitate before determining to rush into the Palace, and naturally have different opinions. A modern playwright would have 'Confused voices', each saying something definite, while interrupting one another. Aeschylus uses this same plan, though he probably made each speak separately without interruption.

1343. ELDERS.

'1. Call the citizens!

2. No—burst in.

3. Yes—do something. Don't lose time.

4. It is obviously a conspiracy.

5. Because we are waiting and they are not.

6. I don't know what to say. No good talking when one cannot act.

7. I agree; we cannot raise him from the dead.

8. Do you mean that we are to submit to these criminals?

9. Intolerable! Better die than submit to tyranny.

10. Are we merely to guess from groans which we have heard that the King is dead?

11. We must know the truth before we get excited.

12. On that we are all agreed: we must find for certain how Agamemnon. . . .' (The sentence appears to be unfinished, a very rare effect.)

Without inquiring into the particular machinery by which the effect was produced, it is clear here that the Elders go up towards the door and are supposed, though the illusion is not maintained afterwards, to enter the room where Clytemnestra stands over the bodies. Really, as they approach

the door, it opens and Clytemnestra is before them,
dominating them and driving them back.

She is possessed by the Daemon of the House
(1475 ff.) and for the moment filled with superhuman strength and pride, which dies down later.
The Elders are overborne by her. Their hot condemnation turns presently into bewilderment.

1372. CLYT. 'Yes; all I said before was a lie.
I hated him, and I have at last killed him. His
blood splashing on my cheek was like the blessed
dew on a parched field.—Which things being so,
my good Elders, you can go your ways and be
happy. For my part I am wild with joy. He has
drunk the cup of curses that he himself filled.'

L. 'We are amazed. The daring of it, to boast
thus over your dead husband!'

CL. 'You try to frighten me, like a witless
woman? My heart beats quite steadily, and I tell
you, in case you do not yet understand, This is
Agamemnon, my husband, killed by my hand;
and rightly killed. That is so.'

The change to lyrics shows a change in the Elders
from definite intention to mere emotion. Clytemnestra does not change.

1407. CH. 'What poison herb have you tasted
to make you mad? You shall be cut off, as you
cut off others, and hated of the people.'

CL. 'Exile and curses for me! Why was there no
harsh word for him when he murdered my child,
Iphigenîa, for 'medicine' against a storm?—As

for threats, I am ready for the battle. Let him who conquers rule!'

CH. 'So proud! It is the blood on your brow makes you mad. But retribution must come. You are friendless, and must some day pay for blow by blow.'

CL. 'Friendless? By all the Powers of Hell, to whom I slew him in sacrifice, I face the future with no fear while Aigisthos lives, my true friend still, as he always has been. This man lies dead—a shield of comfort, that!—this insulter of his wife, this minion of every Chryseis under Troy; and with him his captive prophet-mistress. Both have paid for their wrongs to me.'

Lyric Scene

1448. CH. 'Would I could die, now my kind shepherd is gone, killed by a woman! Alas for Helen, the slayer of many.'

CL. 'Pray not for death; and do not lay the blame on Helen.'

CH. 'O Daemon that fallest upon the house, making women thine instruments! Perched on the dead body like some bird of prey, he calls his fury "Law" (ἐννόμως ὕμνον ὑμνεῖν ἐπεύχεται).'

CL. 'Now you have found the truth! Call on the Daemon of the House. From him comes the ache of the flesh for blood, and ceases not.'

(First sign of weakening; she is beginning to feel 'I cannot have done this.')

CH. 'Indeed, he is very great, and heavy his wrath. Ah me, it is all as Zeus hath willed.'

1489. LAMENT. (Not by the Elders, but by another Chorus of Mourners, perhaps off stage?) 'My King, my King . . . slain in a crafty death, by a wife's hand.'

CL. (She listens and answers the mourners) 'You say I did it? No. Do not imagine that this is I, Clytemnestra. It is the ancient Alastor, the Driver Astray of Atreus who gave the ghastly feast; he has taken upon him the shape of this dead man's wife, and made his sacrifice of atonement, a full-grown King for a child.'

CH. 'You guiltless? No; no one can say that, but the Daemon may have worked with you, forcing his way towards new blood to wash out the old.'

LAMENT. 'My King . . . by a crafty death. . . .'

1523. CL. (As before) 'And was Iphigenîa's not a crafty death? But he cannot boast in Hades. He has got as much as he gave.'

CH. 'I am bewildered, and know not how to think. The rain on the roof affrights me, rain that falls like blood. If it ever abates, it is only fate making ready for the next stroke.'

They begin to see that the death of Agamemnon is not a mere wicked deed; it is the working out of an inevitable law.

1538. LAMENT. 'Would I had died before him. . . . Who shall mourn for him, who in honesty praise him at his tomb?'

CL. (As before) 'What is that to you? By me he fell, by me he died, and by me he shall be buried, not wept by any mere members of his household: is not Iphigenîa waiting by the river of Acheron, to put her arms about him and kiss?'

CH. 'Reviling cometh to meet reviling, and it is hard to pass judgement. The spoiler is despoiled, the slayer slain. While Zeus lives, the Law remains, that *on him that doeth it shall be done.* Who will drive the curse out of this house?' (i.e. I blame nobody. Only let the bloodshed stop.)

1567. CL. 'Now you have found the true law. As for me, I am ready to make treaty with the Daemon of the Pleisthenids; *I will endure this lot, hard as it is to bear,* and He shall depart. I want but a little to live upon, and am now content, *having swept away the madness* wherewith these brethren slew one another.'

The Daemon has faded out of her, her exultation gone. Contrast 1394 and 1571. She is left with only her own strength, exhausted and desiring peace. After this appeal she remains silent till 1654, where she intervenes to appeal again for peace. She does not even answer when addressed 1625. As this scene comes to a quiet close, in bursts AIGISTHOS.

1578. AIGISTHOS. 'Hail, day of Justice! My two brothers were foully murdered by Atreus, this man's father, and I, being spared, was bound to avenge them. Now I have done it, and am content to die.'

An effect such as Euripides loves, of suddenly letting the other side speak. It is called ἀνασκευάσαι τὰ εἰρημένα, shattering the case stated'. This plea is just. Aigisthos is not a mere villain. He has done his duty.

1613. L. 'You admit your guilt? You will be stoned for murder.'

AI. 'Is that the tone you take to your masters? Old men like you are slow at learning, but chains and cold can teach them. Do not kick against the goad, or you will hurt yourself.'

The Leader, baffled by Aigisthos' defence of his action, turns on Clytemnestra, who has no such justification.

1625. L. 'Woman, when your husband was just returned from the war; you whom he trusted as guard of his house, to betray his bed and plot his murder. . . .'

AIG. (interrupting; Clytemnestra is too exhausted to speak) 'That sort of talk too will make trouble. You are not an Orpheus to charm the world. But we will make you obedient to your master.'

1633. L. 'You the master of Argos! You who plotted the murder, and did not dare to do the deed with your own hand!'

AIG. 'To deceive him was obviously his wife's work. I was his old enemy and consequently suspect. However, I have his treasures, and shall do my best to master his subjects. The horse that kicks shall wear a heavy yoke.'

L. 'Coward! If you had this blood-feud, why did you not kill him yourself? You let *his wife help you* (σύν), *which makes a pollution to the earth and its gods.*—Oh, is Orestes somewhere living, to return and kill them both, as they deserve?'

1649. AIG. 'Is that your tone?—Ho, there, my guards!'

Enter a Band of Armed Men, dominating the stage.

L. (to the other Elders). 'Ho, there, your swords!' (Swords are drawn, the old men brave though helpless.)

AIG. 'My sword is drawn too, and I am ready to die.'

L. 'Die then! We accept the omen.'

CLYT. (at last breaking from her long exhausted silence) 'Nay, best-beloved! Let us do no more evil. It is enough as it is. We must not stain ourselves with blood.'

> An extremely interesting line. Apparently she does not feel the slaying of the guilty Agamemnon as a 'stain of blood', and she is longing for peace. To begin slaughtering these innocent Elders would be a different thing. The reading, however, is not certain.

'Back to your houses, ye reverend Elders. Go, before doing leads to suffering. These things we have done had to be. And if now we can say "It is enough", I shall be well content, bruised though I am under the Daemon's heavy heel.—This is the word a woman speaks, if any will listen!'

AIG. 'Are these people to insult me, and mock their master?'

L. 'It is not the way of Argives to fawn on scoundrels.'

AIG. 'Bah, I shall be on your track hereafter!'

L. 'Not if God guides Orestes home.'

AIG. 'Exiles feed on hopes.'

L. 'Go on, wax fat, defiling justice while you can!'

AIG. 'A time will come when you will pay for this.'

L. 'Crow on, like a cock beside his mate.'

CLYT. 'Heed not this vain baying of hounds, *You and I, as rulers in this great House, will order all things well.*'

This is her sincere hope (cf. 1575). We know it cannot be fulfilled.

NOTE

The traditional details of Agamemnon's murder are curiously precise as well as odd in themselves. He was killed in his bath, Ϧροίτη, wrapped in a very long and presumably crimson embroidered robe; he had previously walked Ϧι' ὕβριν on a very long crimson embroidered robe. It is tempting to suggest a hypothesis which would explain all three points. It is known that tombs were often dug up for the sake of plunder. The τυμβωρύχος was a common type of misdoer. Furthermore, a Ἀροίτη, as Wilamowitz has pointed out, can be used either as a bath or a sarcophagus. Suppose in pre-classical days some peasants, of the type to which Greek mythology owes so much, found among the royal tombs at Mycenae a skeleton or mummy wrapped from head to foot in a long and precious embroidery in a marble sarcophagus and showing signs of a violent death. 'A great king', they would say, 'murdered when help-less in his bath, and made more helpless by being wrapped in the great embroidered robe. And why did he deserve death? No doubt he had trampled with impious feet on broideries fit only for the gods.'

INDEX

PRINTED IN
GREAT BRITAIN
AT THE
UNIVERSITY PRESS
OXFORD
BY
CHARLES BATEY
PRINTER
TO THE
UNIVERSITY